The Steroid Deceit

A Body Worth Dying For?

The Steroid Deceit

A Body Worth Dying For?

Jeff Rutstein

Custom Fitness Publishing
Boston, Massachusetts

The Steroid Deceit: A Body Worth Dying For?

Published by
  Custom Fitness Publishing
  75 Saint Alphonsus St., Suite G
  Boston, Massachusetts 02120
  1-800-374-9959
  www.steroiddeceit.com
  www.jeffrutstein.com

Edited by Alan Russell
Cover art by John Warner
Cover layout and interior design and layout by
  Robert Goodman, Silvercat™, San Diego, California

Publisher's Cataloging in Publication Data

Rutstein, Jeffrey S.
   The steroid deceit : a body worth dying for? / Jeff Rutstein,
-- 1st ed. -- Boston, Mass. : Custom Fitness, 2005.

   p. ; cm.
   ISBN: 0-9760170-2-4
   ISBN-13: 978-0-9760170-2-8

   1. Anabolic steroids--Health aspects. 2. Steroids--Physiological effect.
3. Doping in sports. 4. Body image. 5. Substance abuse.
I. Title.

RC1230.R83 2005
615/.704--dc22   0506

Printed in the United States of America

To my two children,
Ryan and Michael,
who are my little miracles.
They have inspired me
throughout this process

Contents

Preface

Having abused steroids for three and one half years during the mid-to-late 1980s, I know the detrimental effects of those illegal drugs all too well. During that time the use of steroids was widespread; nowadays it is far greater. Steroid use goes well beyond professional sports and athletics. It is now found in every community and school. Too many teenagers think steroid use is innocuous, and take them like they would aspirin in the hopes of having a "cut" or "bulked up" body.

It was a child that pointed out the Emperor wasn't wearing any clothes. What adults don't see, kids do. Our children can identify who uses steroids. Certain professional athletes might deny their involvement with steroids, but the kids aren't blind to the results. Having once idolized sports figures and bodybuilders, I know the not-so-hidden message that steroid use is sending our children. I was a steroid user for years, and started using them as an impressionable teen.

Steroids almost killed me. For a time I was ashamed to talk about my past, but now I feel it's my mission to speak out so as to prevent others from making the mistakes that I made. I want my story to dissuade those considering using steroids from starting, and for those who are already using steroids, I hope my words help you to quit.

You might be asking yourself, why should I listen to this guy? He's not some big name athlete, or a movie star, or a rock musician. That's all very true. I am someone like you, and if I can help you avoid all the pitfalls and suffering I experienced, then everything I went through will have been worth it. I have attended the funerals of users and know the devastating effects firsthand. Enough is enough.

The skeptical reader is saying, "That couldn't happen to me." There was a time when I would have been skeptical, but that was a time before I started using steroids. Unfortunately, all the available statistics show that steroid use in this country is going up. There's a lot of advertising that glorifies the use of "juice." It's hard to counter that kind of barrage, but I tell people that what they are seeing is a noose, not juice.

I wish the recent Congressional hearings on steroid abuse had taken place many years ago. Seeing the pain of the parents whose children passed away from steroid abuse reminded me of the agony that my father went through as I was withdrawing from those illegal drugs. He knew that I had lost the will to live, and he didn't know how to pull me out of that black hole that was consuming me. There were many times that I hoped I wouldn't wake up, but as bad as I looked during my long recovery period, my father looked worse. Now that I am the father of two young boys, I don't want any other family to have to go through the pain that my family and others have endured.

This book provides some ugly truth. And, no, it's not as pretty as pictures of smiling bodybuilders with huge shoulders and massive pecs, but I don't want it to be. What I'm going to do is pull back the "muscle curtain" and show you the world of steroids, letting you see what is illusion, and what is truth.

꙯ Jeff Rutstein

Acknowledgments

Dr. Harrison Pope, for his groundbreaking research in the field of anabolic steroids.

Kevin Meehan, who helped me see the larger picture, and has always taken the time to give advice.

Alan Russell, who has been the best editor one can imagine.

Tom Campbell, who helped steer me in the right direction and was willing to hear me out.

Antoinette and Jared Kuritz, for encouraging me to take on this important topic and creating a marketing vision.

Bob Goodman, for his interior design and laying out and turning my words into a book.

John Warner, for creating such a wonderful cover design.

My mother, who has been my biggest fan and supporter.

Lastly, to my wife Kerry for understanding the importance of this project.

1

The Man in the Mirror

As Gregor Samsa awoke one morning from uneasy dreams he found himself transformed in his bed into a gigantic insect.

✂ Franz Kafka, *The Metamorphosis*

The party was getting louder, but I wasn't adding much to the volume. The New Year was about to arrive, and I was facing that prospect with a lot more dread than glee. I hadn't wanted to be alone, so I was at a nightclub hoping for safety in numbers. But I felt alone anyway. The witching hour had almost arrived and everyone's eyes were on the television. The ball atop One Times Square was being readied for its big splash. The ghosts of coaches past were in my ear: *Keep your eye on the ball*, they'd always yelled. I watched the ball, but what I was really thinking about was my New Year's resolution.

I am going to quit taking steroids, I told myself. This is it, I vowed. I was serious about my good intentions, but then I had been serious before. When I first started taking anabolic steroids I had told myself it would only be for six weeks. That had been three and a half years before. Since that time I had tried quitting a number of times only to go back to them.

Like Mark Twain said, "Quitting smoking is easy. I've done it hundreds of times." Quitting steroids was like that for me. I would stop using them but then start up again. I was afraid of the consequences of taking steroids but even more afraid of shrinking away without them. My fake muscles were my self esteem. What I didn't know was that my house of cards was about to fall apart.

Mirror watching is one of the great pastimes of body builders. It is the rare reflection that they can walk by without posing, and I was no exception. After using steroids for several years, along with working with weights, I had the body of a musclehead. I was five foot six inches tall, but weighed one hundred and ninety pounds, with overdeveloped chest, shoulders, and upper arms. At the time, my whole life was based on my physique. Because of that, whenever I tried discontinuing steroids it always made me depressed. On those occasions when I stopped using, my mirror watching would make me anxious and upset for I could see my muscles shrinking. For me, that was like losing a limb, and the next thing I knew I was using again to regain that bulk.

But not this time, I told myself. This was one New Year's resolution I was going to keep. I was going to get off the juice and quit forever. Before doing so, though, I had opted for a big send-off. Several hours earlier I had injected myself with a mega-dose of testosterone. In my years of using steroids I had been taking a veritable cocktail, including Dianabol, Deca-Durabolin, Testosterone propionate, Equipoise, Winstrol, and Sustanon. But now that was all behind me, I told myself.

The party was getting louder with the anticipation of New Year's spreading a fever to the revelers. A casual acquaintance I knew approached me and said, "Hey, you're looking good, Jeff."

In my case I knew that seeing was not believing. I wanted to believe in what the mirror was showing me, but I couldn't. My body was big, but I knew I was a balloon with a leak. I didn't want to live a lie anymore. Somewhere deep down I knew my life of deception was killing me.

"So what are you lifting?" my friend asked.

I went into my gym talk patter, bragging about how I had bench pressed 225 pounds 27 times and done some reps with 350 pounds or more. It was easy to escape that way. When it came to escaping from reality, I was a Houdini. Although I was about to graduate from the University of Massachusetts at Amherst with a degree in economics, most of my college experience had been spent in the weightroom instead of the classroom. Truth to tell, I was terrified at the prospect of going out into the real world. My parents had spent good money for me to go to school and had no idea their son was a junkie whose drug of choice was anabolic steroids. I was so scared of leaving my artificial world that I had convinced my parents that I needed to take some more courses.

The friend drifted away. When it came down to it, I really didn't have much to say. I had become a meathead. I didn't like myself, so it was self-fulfilling to not have others like me. My relationships with women rarely lasted more than a date or two. Some of them would tell me how strong I looked, but I felt anything but that. My body was a total mask; the muscles hid how weak I was. I usually acted like a total jackass with women, treating them like dirt so as to sabotage any chance of a relationship. In spite of the muscles I felt self-conscious. Because of the steroid use, my testicles were no bigger than grapes. Testicular atrophy is just one of the wonderful byproducts of steroid use.

"Ten, nine . . ."

The countdown had started, and everyone but me seemed to be smiling and happy. Couples were already locking lips, ready to bring in the New Year's with a kiss.

I thought of my resolution and how I had gotten where I was. It hadn't been that long ago that I had never even heard of steroids. I first became acquainted with these drugs after my friend Mark and I joined a local gym. The idea at the time was that we would work with weights so as to look buff and impress women. Mark and I didn't have any proper training, so we just went from machine to machine doing haphazard workouts. From the first, though, we lingered to watch the muscleheads.

"I want to look like those guys," I said, and Mark echoed his agreement.

We started spending more time at the gym and hung around the bodybuilders as much as we could. Occasionally they would throw us a bone, telling us how to do an exercise or work a repetition. Mark and I kept flailing about with the weights, but we didn't see much in the way of improvement. Try as we might, our bodies weren't looking anything like these guys. Eventually, though, the muscleheads let us in on their little secret: they were taking something called steroids.

It was a club that we wanted to join, no questions asked. The idea of getting muscles seemed like a no-brainer. At the time, Mark and I didn't think to ask if there would be any ramifications from these drugs we wanted to take. The only thing we wanted to know was where we could get them.

"Eight, seven . . ."

While people at the party were raising their glasses, I was looking into mine. My glass was empty, and so was I. I stared a little deeper into it, and my looking glass took me back to a time when I ventured out to get steroids with Mark. We had already done a few cycles from steroids purchased from a dealer at the gym, but now we were moving on to a "legitimate" supplier.

The muscleheads had told us about a doctor who would write prescriptions for us, no questions asked. Our gym "doctor," Big Bob, had told us what we should get and the doses we should administer to ourselves.

Our Dr. "Feelgood" had an office near Amherst that wasn't far from campus, although the neighborhood was in a shady part of town. At the time it was a rush to be slumming for steroids and only added to our excitement. Mark and I thought this was all a great adventure. The first time we stepped into Dr. "Feelgood's" waiting room, we thought we were on another planet. Most of those waiting to see the doctor were junkies, and some were clearly under the influence. There were others who appeared ill at ease and anxious, individuals clearly in need of a "fix." Some people around us were snoozing, while others were amped, talking a mile a minute, and still others were carrying on conversations with themselves.

Amidst all the dregs and outcasts, though, Mark and I saw a very attractive looking woman. Both of us headed over in her direction and managed to get seats on either side of her. Being young and dumb, most of our attention was focused on the woman's large chest. Our eyes must have finally gone north, for we ended up striking a conversation with her. Mark and I each tried to outdo the other. Each of us was hoping to get her name or number, but before we got too far our busty friend was called in to see the doctor.

When she was out of sight, I told Mark that he might as well give up, because she only had eyes for me. Mark told me that I was crazy, and that he wouldn't be surprised if he hooked up with her before she left.

One of the junkies woke up long enough to take pity on our stupidity. "He's a she," he said.

In outraged unison, Mark and I said, "What?"

"The doc gives her drugs," the junkie said. "It's like hormone replacement or something that makes him look more like a her."

The junkie didn't waste any more words on us. I got the feeling he thought we were too stupid to even try and panhandle from. His head nodded off, and Mark and I looked at each with stunned glances. Too late, we started putting together the clues. Our woman did have a deep voice, and she had worn an awful lot of makeup. Come to think of it, I remembered how she had large hands and feet.

The two of us grew very quiet, and our argument never resumed. We stopped bragging about which of us she liked more. That was something we each would have been glad to concede to the other.

"Six, five . . ."

Everyone else at the party was yelling out the countdown. My eyes wandered over to an attractive girl who had caught my eye earlier. She was with her girlfriend, and both of them were calling out the countdown together.

I looked at her a little more critically. Yes, she was a real girl. Once burned . . .

The doctor didn't look much better than his patients. He was unshaven and had a world-weariness that made me tired just looking at him. His practice seemed based on writing prescriptions as fast as he could. No one was ever in his office more than five minutes.

Dr. "Feelgood" asked us what we wanted. He didn't inquire about why we wanted the steroids; enough muscleheads already visited him so that he was familiar with the routine.

The only problem he had with making out our prescriptions was getting the right spelling.

I said we needed some Dianabol.

He nodded and started jotting. "Is that b-a-l-l?" he asked.

I corrected his spelling. In subsequent visits his spelling never got any better. Mark and I always coached him on how to spell, and with his shaky hand he'd scrawl the words we so wanted.

"Four, three . . ."

The shouting at the party was reaching a crescendo. People were blowing on horns and noisemakers were being shaken and rattled.

Unexpectedly, I remembered my college roommate's favorite toast: "Eat, drink and be merry, for tomorrow you may die."

At that moment, those words resonated through my head.

The pharmacy that filled our steroid fix was in an even seedier part of town. The first few times we picked up our prescriptions, we felt awkward and uneasy going there. Mark and I had been raised in Randolph, a nice Boston suburb. We had caring parents and middle class values. At the onset of our steroid use, what we were doing felt wrong.

"It's only for six weeks, though," I rationalized to Mark, and he was quick to agree.

Our great plan was to do a "cycle" of steroids. We figured it would be like getting a summer tan. All we were going to do was put on some muscles. Of course, to obtain these results meant doing some things we had never done before. When it came time to inject my first needle, I was too afraid to do it. Big Bob the gym doctor was the one who had to dart (meathead slang for inject) me.

Unfortunately, my fears didn't last. All too soon I became adept at poking myself in the thigh and not even thinking about what I was doing.

The results, and my addiction, were almost immediate. In that first six week period I put on twenty pounds of what I thought was muscle. I would look in the mirror, and see the results. I had muscles, and I thought that made me a real man. At the end of six weeks I did stop, but not for long. I couldn't stand the idea of "deflating." I didn't want to lose this new-found power.

I'll do it another six weeks, I decided. The self-deception began to get easier and easier as time passed, until finally I couldn't tell a lie from the truth, and I didn't even want to make any distinction between the two.

"Two, one . . ."

Someone exploded a cork from a champagne bottle, and bubbly shot out. People were jumping up and down. One group was singing:
Should auld acquaintance be forgot,
And never brought to mind,
Should auld acquaintance be forgot,
And auld lang syne.

Auld lang syne translates to "times gone by." It was time for out with the old and in with the new. That was what I wanted more than anything else, although anyone looking at me might have wondered why. The steroids had delivered. I weighed 190 pounds and I was that image I had always wanted. So why was it that I was so desperate to give up the juice?

A major part of that impetus came from Adriana DiGrande, a speech therapist who had helped me with my stutter during my time at college. Because I worked so closely with Adriana, her opinion mattered greatly to me. She had helped me overcome my fear of speaking; Adriana was my confessor and rock. I was used to her being positive and cheerful, so when she confronted me during winter break I was shocked.

In her most severe voice, Adriana said, "Jeff, why don't you grow up? You need to go to a treatment center." If I didn't, Adriana warned, I was going to die.

I needed that dose of tough love. I had thought I could hide my steroid and alcohol and drug abuse from everyone. They say the best mirror is an old friend. Adriana was the best mirror. Of course she didn't tell me anything that I didn't already know. When I was a little boy there were a series of margarine commercials featuring a woman who was supposed to be Mother Nature. While eating what she thought was butter, and extolling its virtues, Mother Nature was told it was margarine. That didn't go over well. In a fit of pique, she would say, "It's not nice to fool Mother Nature!"

Lightning would flash and the pastoral scene would quickly change to one of chaos and discord.

I hadn't fooled Adriana, and I hadn't fooled Mother Nature. In fact, Mother Nature was about to strike back at me in all sorts of ways. Little did I know that real lightning bolts were about to rain down on me.

The ball descended down the pole. New Year's was here.

This time I won't drop the ball, I promised. I am done with steroids.

At that moment, in the midst of all the merriment and celebrating, I had no idea what the next year would bring. Had I known, I probably would have run from the party screaming.

2

The Witch's Brew

Eye of newt, and toe of frog, wool of bat, and tongue of dog.

❧ Shakespeare, *macbeth*

Since I had made my own body a Petri dish, I shouldn't have been surprised at the consequences. Like every other young person, though, I had this false sense of immortality. Dying was for other people.

At the time I was taking steroids, I had no idea of the consequences of the drugs I was putting into my body. Only after the fact did I learn about the witch's brew that I was swallowing and injecting into me.

Testosterone is a male sex hormone. As its name suggests, it is a hormone that is mostly produced in the testes (the adrenal glands also produce some). Of all male hormones, it is the most biologically active. Testosterone stimulates the sexual development of males and their secondary sexual characteristics such as facial hair, a deeper voice, greater muscle mass, and heavier bone structure. It is testosterone which masculinizes the brain in male fetuses. In females, testosterone is mostly produced in the ovaries. The sex drive of both men and woman is strongly influenced by testosterone.

In the 1930s European scientists created a synthetic form of testosterone. This synthetic hormone was used to treat hypogonadism, a condition in which the testes don't produce enough natural testosterone. The creation and use of synthetic testosterone helped the physical and sexual development of males deficient in testosterone. Like so many drugs, though, synthetic testosterone began to be abused. As they say, the road to hell was paved with good intentions.

The Germans began using testosterone during World War II. It was administered in the infirmary to help the sick and weak gain weight, as well as to stave off malnutrition. Some also affirm that testosterone was administered to soldiers to increase their strength and aggressiveness.

From the fields of war steroids started to be found on playing fields. Perhaps it's no wonder that the Duke of Wellington once said of his victory over Napoleon, "The Battle of Waterloo was won on the playing fields of Eton." Trying to get an edge over your opponent on both the sporting field and battlefield has been going on since time immemorial. Greek wrestlers supposedly ate the testicles of sheep to build muscle; Norse warriors (not called the Berserkers for nothing) ate hallucinogenic mushrooms; Australian aborigines chewed the pituri plant. It isn't scientifically known whether eating sheep testicles improves athletic performance, but it didn't take long to prove that anabolic steroids did work.

When the Russians scored impressive victories in weightlifting and strength events in the 1956 Olympics, it wasn't only the sporting world that took notice. In 1958 Dr. John Ziegler, the physician for the U.S. weight-lifting team, developed an anabolic steroid for athletes. Male sex steroids are called androgens. It is these androgens that control the development of masculine characteristics in vertebrates: deer develop antlers; baboons get large canine teeth; men get larger muscle mass. Today there are more than a hundred different types of anabolic steroids that were derived from, or based on, testosterone.

For years I had hit the juice in six to twelve week periods of "cycles," increasing the dosage and then tapering down. I would then take three or four weeks off before starting another cycle. Like most steroid users, I combined or "stacked" different injectables with steroid pills during my cycle, trying to achieve just the right combination of drugs and dosages from my "gym doctor" Big Bob. The way I listened to him, you would have thought he had graduated summa cum laude from Harvard Medical School. I am sure that if he had told me eating cow manure would have increased the size of my biceps, I would have rushed out to the nearest farm with a shovel.

I had the misplaced notion that "gym doctors" had all the answers, and that there was a right and wrong way to do steroids. The truth of the matter is that there is no right way, just degrees of abuse. Some steroid users take a little poison, some a lot. Like many other steroid abusers, I was routinely taking dosages a hundred times greater than would have been prescribed for any medical condition. There has never been a shortage of misinformation about "safe ways" to take steroids. There is no safe way.

They say the bigger you are, the harder you fall. I ended up falling farther than I would have thought possible. There had been warning signs before: blood rushing from my nose and mouth; insomnia; depression; irritability; irrational behavior. All of those just proved to be minor symptoms, though. The real fallout was about to begin.

It happened almost immediately after New Year's. I stayed true to my resolution, even though it almost killed me. The testosterone that was in my system triggered what mental health professionals would describe as a "manic episode." For six weeks I barely slept or ate. I had incredible, if misused, energy. At that time the only thing I knew about was working out. I got this notion in my head that I would be this guru and personal trainer to the stars and began working night and day setting up a business I called Ultimate Physique. Luckily, I didn't get very far with that, saving any potential clients from my insanity. The only thing about workouts that I knew was *no pain, no gain*. The working name for that business should have been "Meathead Physique."

I decided I needed a fancy car to help me with my grandiose scheme, so I went to a car dealer and picked out my luxury model. The only problem with that idea was that I had about three dollars to my name. When the car dealer checked on my resources and found I had no money, he told me the bad news: no car. That wasn't an answer I wanted to hear. I started babbling about Ultimate Physique, and that sure wasn't something he wanted to hear. Several employees had to forcibly escort me out of the showroom.

During that time I didn't like looking at the mirror. It was almost as if my body was betraying me. I was losing weight and muscle at a rapid rate. By the time I hit bottom, I had lost more than forty pounds, going from 190 to 145. But that wasn't my biggest loss.

In addition to losing weight, I lost my mind.

In retrospect, I shouldn't have been surprised. I had been relying on artificial drugs to pump testosterone into my veins. I didn't have any need for balls, and that's why they had shrunk so during my usage; I was ingesting and injecting massive quantities of testosterone and didn't need to produce it on my own. For years my moods had been regulated by an artificial regimen. I had put myself in the ultimate Catch-22: without muscles I thought I was nothing; with steroid muscles I was slowly but surely killing myself.

My parents witnessed my manic episode. For them it was a nightmare. The boy they loved became a crazed stranger right in front of their eyes. Fearing for my life, my father finally called the police. When they arrived on the front doorstep of our house and began questioning me I kept asking them, "What do you want?" It didn't take them long to determine that I needed to come with them. That wasn't something I wanted to do, but they didn't give me a choice.

They took me to Pembroke Psychiatric Hospital. I didn't go quietly. I was screaming bloody murder, trying to get anyone to listen to me. I kept yelling that they had made a terrible mistake. When I was put into a holding room, I really lost it. Time and again I threw myself against the door. I was absolutely determined to break it down. Whether I would have succeeded I don't know, for suddenly the door opened and I was rushed by several big men. In moments they threw me to the ground and forcibly held me down until a doctor injected me with a drug that knocked me out. It wasn't the last time they had to do that to me. Besides being out of my mind, I was a slow learner.

I had been at Pembroke for several days before I got the opportunity to use a payphone. I immediately called the police and informed them, "Hey, you have to come and get me. I'm being held prisoner." The dispatcher started talking to me and I began to babble, telling him that I had been kidnapped and that there had been a miscarriage of justice. I must not have been nearly as persuasive as I thought I was because the dispatcher finally said, "Hey, there's a reason you're at Pembroke. You're nuts." And then he hung up on me.

It was a succinct psychiatric evaluation; unfortunately it was also an accurate one. I was nuts.

I stayed at Pembroke for a month. I think I was finally let out because I stopped being violent. The bad thing about what hospital officials thought was my improved behavior was that my lethargy masked my growing despair. The reason I wasn't acting out was that I didn't have the energy. But as bad as I was feeling, I still wasn't close to rock bottom.

Steroids give you a feeling of false invincibility. The muscles that they produce look and feel real, but I knew they were just an illusion. Without any testosterone coursing through me, I began to feel more husk than human. Looking at the mirror only confirmed my fears: I saw a wasted and worthless human being staring back.

After I returned home from Pembroke I was floored by depression. When I say floored, I mean that quite literally. I couldn't move. I didn't leave my bed. I sank into an abyss that only went down and down and didn't offer any hope of escape. There was no light at the end of my tunnel. I was without hope or purpose. The worst thing about my situation was that I was so numb it felt as if I wasn't alive, so dead inside I was sure I had become a zombie, shuffling around in the world of the living, but not one of them.

The only reason I didn't commit suicide was that I never could quite get enough energy to do it; killing myself just seemed too much of a bother. What I wanted most was to not wake up. When my body didn't cooperate and expire on its own, I finally decided that I would take some pills and be done with it. My parents surprised me in the middle of that act by coming home early, and my father saw my hand was filled with pills.

"What are you doing?" he shouted.

I didn't have the strength to explain, but I was angry that I couldn't just die and be done with it. With a rare burst of energy I tossed the pills on the floor, and then I went back to doing what I did best during my black funk– staying in bed and doing nothing.

For much of my life I remember being depressed, but this was a clinical depression that hung my soul out to dry. It was like nothing I have ever felt before or since, and I pray it never happens again. Not too long ago I was hospitalized and had to have my appendix removed. I heard from a lot of well-wishers, and all the while I wanted to tell them, "This is nothing." For me, it was almost a luxury to feel pain, especially as I remembered what it was like to feel nothing, and be totally bereft of spirit. I had never understood the expression that it's better to feel pain than to feel nothing until I experienced my year in the bottomless pit.

Coming off steroids, my situation was compounded by getting hooked on prescription drugs. I desperately wanted to find relief for my situation and went in search of a legal fix. To help me get through my funk I found a doctor who prescribed Xanax and in short order I became an addict. I was the one who asked the doctor for the Xanax, even though I didn't know very much about the drug or the side effects that came from taking it. I went from one poison to another, and I can't tell you which was worse.

Once again, I had to be hospitalized. This time I went to the Newton Wellesley Hospital. I had seen the movie *One Flew Over the Cuckoo's Nest,* and now I got to live it. The cast of characters around me was a lot wilder than anything Ken Kesey ever wrote about. There was a man there who said he was Jesus; another who thought he was a vampire. There were screamers and patients that needed to be restrained from hurting themselves or others; there were those who suffered in complete silence, and catatonic cases that you swore didn't even move an eyelash. In the midst of all that, there was a 'roid head hooked on Xanax. Maybe my fellow patients thought I was worse than they were, and maybe they were right.

When I arrived at Newton Wellesley I came off taking eight milligrams of Xanax at a time. An elephant shouldn't take eight milligrams of Xanax. Because I had gone to a few AA meetings, I was convinced that I should go cold turkey, just as I had with the steroids. What I didn't know, or couldn't understand, was that going cold turkey with my Xanax addiction would likely have resulted in my death. The doctors said I needed to take medication to stay alive. I'm not sure if I wanted to die, or if was stubborn, or maybe I was just stupid – it was probably a combination of all three – but I refused the meds. Once again the goon squad was called in to manhandle me, and I was shot up with something. When I awakened, I was strapped to the bed.

I remained at Newton Wellesley for two weeks. When I had first visited "Dr. Feelgood" to get my steroid prescription, I felt superior to the "freak show" around me. Now I was a member in good standing in that community. Steroids had made me a junkie who regularly inserted a two inch needle into my flesh. I wasn't any better than the abusers and crazies; I was one of them.

My recovery was slow. I was sent to Pembroke Hospital once again to fight my addictions and demons. When I returned home, I started going to AA meetings regularly. I associated my drinking with steroid use. Often I drank heavily to take the edge off what I was putting into my body. Steroids never made me feel comfortable in my own skin, and I suppose there was a good reason for that – I knew my muscles were borrowed and not earned. I had a psychological addiction to steroids, and I could and did talk about that at the meetings.

Like any addict, I felt the pull of my drug of choice. Whenever I looked at my body I was dissatisfied, and couldn't help but remember how I had appeared when taking steroids. There was this sense that I had given up my powers, like Superman being confronted by kryptonite.

I stayed true to my New Year's resolution, though. As depressed and battered as I was, I still knew that steroids had gotten me into this mess. I also knew with a grim certainty that steroids would kill me if I started up my cycling again. At the time there didn't seem to be any evidence for this. No one had linked steroids with depression, and the phrase "roid rage" hadn't even been created. The only thing I had to go on was a gut feeling that made me turn away from the Siren's song to come back to steroids.

That song is being sung even louder today to too many impressionable ears. The lyrics haven't changed: Take me, and you'll look powerful; I am your shortcut to a better world; I can be your self-esteem, I can be your everything.

It took me some time to put that chorus behind me. When I gave up steroids I lost a year of my life. It was a small enough price, I suppose. I lived, while others who have walked my same path were not as fortunate.

Still, to this day I think about all the things I could have been doing with my life during the three and a half years I used steroids, and the one year I traveled around in hell trying to find a way out.

The Good Looking Corpse

Things are seldom as they seem, Skim milk masquerades as cream.

⇛ William Schwenck Gilbert, *H.M.S. Pinafore*

Too often you hear young people say, "I want to live fast, die young, and leave a good looking corpse." It's no wonder that steroids have a particular appeal to the young, as most youths can't even imagine themselves being middle-aged. Because the future isn't something they dwell upon, teens find it hard to conceive of the steroid related ailments that come over time. When you only consider the here and now, you don't worry about paying the piper in the future. Because of that, steroids have a fast track appeal to many kids. They view them as a shortcut to a ripped body. What I tell teenagers is that if they truly do want to live fast, die young, and leave a good looking corpse, then there probably is no better way of accomplishing that than through steroids.

Like many kids, when I was growing up I didn't feel comfortable in my own skin. It's not surprising that so many teenagers want to assume another body that they think steroids can provide. I wasn't very happy growing up. I had a stuttering problem that made me self-conscious and a target for others. My elementary school teacher used to have us call out our math grades so that she could record the scores. On one occasion I had received a ninety on a test, but when it was my turn to announce my score I called out, "Sixty." The reason I shortchanged myself was that I had trouble saying any word that began with "n." I was so terrified of others teasing me about my stuttering that I would rather look stupid than speech impaired.

It also didn't help that I was small. Class bullies liked to pick on me. This feeling of being targeted played heavily on me, and it often left me feeling utterly despondent. What I didn't know at the time is that I wasn't alone in having these feelings; countless studies show that a high percentage of teenagers are unhappy and have low self-esteem. If you ask any adult what was the most miserable time of their life, the majority will single out their adolescence.

Steroids primarily appeal to two categories of young people: those looking for a boost in their self-esteem, and those looking for an edge in sports. Both groups want to supersize themselves. They see steroids as a ticket to being noticed and to somehow being new and improved.

I suppose that it's not surprising that a stuttering, small kid with low self-esteem was attracted to steroids. Instead of dealing with my issues, I thought it would be easier to run away from them. In that regard, I certainly wasn't unique. Modern technology is allowing for brain mapping and a better understanding of brain chemistry. Recent studies suggest that teen brains aren't developed enough to make "mature" decisions. Brain scans show that in teenagers the right ventrial striatum is underactive, which makes it extremely difficult for teens to perceive long-term goals. The teen brain wants an immediate reward. To young minds, steroids fit that bill far more than hard work and perseverance. Worrying about the dangers of steroid usage just doesn't occur to them. The teenage mantra might as well be, "Damn the torpedoes, full speed ahead."

Like many others, my youthful heroes were larger than life. I loved comic book characters with their rippling muscles and their powers. I could fantasize about how it would be if I was The Incredible Hulk or The Mighty Thor. For many years I idolized football players like Lyle Alzado and other bulked up heroes of the gridiron. I thought muscles commanded respect. For a long time I even had a poster of Arnold Schwarzenegger hanging over my bed. My mother commented on the poster one time, saying "Doesn't he look ridiculous?" I couldn't believe that's what she really thought, just as she couldn't believe that I wanted to look like Arnold.

Brain chemistry/maturity isn't the only factor that comes into play when it comes to teens choosing to use steroids. Every day Americans are bombarded with advertisements foisting images of beauty upon us. These communications come to us over television, radio, magazines, billboards, and newspapers. On any given day we can see up to 600 such messages, many of them telling us we need to be fit and beautiful.

This constant barrage has resulted in a number of dangerous behaviors. At first it was thought that it was mainly girls and women that were falling prey to the pressures of looking good and trying to live up to impossible standards. More and more there were stories of females falling victim to these insidious traps. When public figures like Karen Carpenter actually died, the words bulimia and anorexia became part of the public lexicon. But as it turns out, it is not only women who suffer a distorted perception of their own body image.

Recent studies have revealed that men have been suffering similar fixations, and their trying to achieve this ideal has put them at ever greater risk. There are a number of parallels to behaviors associated with bulimia and anorexia and those associated with steroid use. To make people understand my own affliction I often tell them that I had "Bigorexia." That usually gets a laugh, but it also gives others an understanding of what I was dealing with. A woman with anorexia needs to waste away to try and achieve what she perceives to be an acceptable body image. Harrison G. Pope, M.D., of Harvard University (and one of the co-authors of *The Adonis Complex*), described what I was going through as reverse anorexia. I needed to get bigger and bigger. And just as anorexia often leads to serious health issues, so does reverse anorexia.

Recent scientific studies have documented a growing male obsession with their bodies. Dr. Pope, along with fellow psychiatrist Dr. Katharine Phillips, and psychologist Roberto Olivardia, wrote their breakthrough book *The*

Adonis Complex that details this new health crisis affecting males.

Among their alarming findings:

+ Over one million and as many as three million American males have taken anabolic steroids or other illegal growth enhancing drugs to look better
+ Eating disorders are becoming ever more prevalent among males
+ At least a million men have developed body dysmorphic disorder and exhibit an obsessive preoccupation with what they perceive are flaws in their appearance.

Pope, Phillips and Olivardia's findings speak to my own experiences. While I was telling people I had "Bigorexia," these researchers were documenting muscle dysmorphia, a syndrome where males, no matter how big or well built they might be, don't think they are muscular enough. Just as an emaciated person with anorexia nervosa looks in the mirror and sees a heavy image, so do these men look into a mirror and see a frail and weak person staring back at them.

The authors of *The Adonis Complex* chose the name Adonis from Greek mythology. Adonis was half man and half god, and the ultimate hunk; even the goddesses swooned when they saw him. Throughout the centuries painters have tried to capture the looks and body of Adonis. As much as these artists exaggerated his musculature, the

Adonis of portraits looks anemic standing next to some of the huge steroid filled bodybuilders of today.

Taking a name from Greek Mythology isn't anything new for bodybuilders. Angelo Charles Siciliano became known as Charles Atlas. For many decades Atlas advertisements ran in comic books under the caption, "I was a 97 pound weakling." Beneath that pronouncement was the picture of a muscular Charles Atlas, as well as a cartoon caption showing how when he was young a bully kicked sand in his face when he was with a girl on the beach at Coney Island. The weakling couldn't do anything about it; the transformed Atlas could. Generations of youth aspired to attaining the body of Charles Atlas (he won the title of "The World's Most Perfectly Developed Man" in the 1920s). Nowadays there are high school kids with bodies more muscular than Atlas's. Not coincidentally, those teens are using steroids.

The Atlas advertisements were written for kids like me. I was afraid of having sand kicked in my face. I was scared of being seen as weak. A favorite male expression is to say, "I'd give my left nut for that." Usually they're talking about a particular car, or woman, or experience. To get muscles, I almost did give my left nut.

Now that advertisers have learned that men are every bit as vulnerable to their own body insecurities as are women, billion dollar industries have grown up pushing body supplements, penile growth products, cosmetics, and hair-loss treatments, to name but a few. The steroid industry has grown as well, benefiting from this new climate promoting masculine fears.

The messages are starting at an ever younger age. The Adonis Complex is fueled by modern culture. Open a magazine, play a videogame, look at a comic book, and you'll see ever bigger muscles and the glorification of larger than life males. Barbie now has competition in G.I. Joe. Despite Barbie's popularity, for years critics have derided her "impossible" anatomy. Some have even suggested that there should be a "normal figure" Barbie doll. If Barbie was a life-sized woman, there have been different estimates as to what her figure would be, but all agree even a supermodel wouldn't come close. G.I. Joe and other male action figures are now vying with Barbie with their unrealistic physiques. It wasn't always that way. There was a time when G.I. Joe had a normal physique. With each incarnation, though, G.I. Joe has become larger and larger. Such long time comic book heroes as Batman and Superman are also much more muscular. Boys are getting the message that bigger is better, and it certainly doesn't stop with action figures or superheroes.

Madison Avenue and Hollywood are powerful influences. Their "gospel" is seen on a daily basis in hundreds of ways, and by the yardsticks they have been promoting "measuring up" has never been so impossible. Of course there is a reason for that. Long ago steroid use escaped the weightroom and found new homes in endeavors far afoot from athletics. Actors and models started taking steroids to look bigger and more cut, and those images have permeated throughout our culture. It should surprise no one, then, that the percentage of American men dissatisfied with their bodies is now higher than it has ever been. A 1997 study discovered that 45% of American men were unhappy with their muscle tone, almost double the percentage of those who reported being unhappy in the same survey only 25 years earlier.

Adults aren't the only ones dissatisfied with their body image. The U.S. Center of Disease Control and Prevention believes that 6-11% of high-school males, and 2-5% of high-school females, currently use steroids. That means between half a million and one million high school students have abused steroids, with the number growing each year. We used to worry about our children being able to handle too much sugar. Do we think their minds and bodies are somehow more ready to handle massive doses of testosterone?

Contrary to what many think, the steroid problem isn't a new one. In 1988 the Journal of the American Medical Association studied more than three thousand twelfth-grade males throughout the United States and reported that 6.6% of the boys said they had used anabolic steroids. That translated to a figure of one boy in 15 using steroids. More recent studies have shown that this figure has either remained constant or grown.

When I was informed of these statistics, I wished I could have said I was surprised, but I wasn't. Children have grown up hearing the message that drugs and alcohol are bad and have been made aware of the serious health consequences that can occur from abusing drugs. Countless millions of dollars have been spent spreading anti-drug messages, while at the same time steroids have received almost a free pass. Indeed, the use of steroids has even been glorified.

Duke Nukem is one of the most popular videogames ever produced. The games, like Duke, have become bigger and badder over time. In *Duke Nukem 3D*, and *Duke Nukem Total Meltdown,* steroids have been introduced as incentives. Players are advised that if they, "Collect STEROIDS you will be incredibly fast and strong (your kick will be lethal) for a short period of time."

Hey, if "Earth's last chance" (as Duke is portrayed) can use steroids to his advantage, then why shouldn't the kids who play the game?

It's not only arcade characters like Duke that have influenced kids. The use of steroids in professional sports seems to have reached epidemic proportions. All too often it seems to be the rule rather than the exception that players in the National Football League and Major League Baseball use steroids. The filter down effect is being felt not only in college ranks, but in high school. If it's perceived that the "big boys" need steroids, it is easy to see why those in the junior ranks also feel the pressure to use.

Looking as good as possible now seems to have become the national pastime. Cosmetic surgery procedures continue to increase in popularity. In 2003 there were 8.7 million procedures performed, up 33% from the year before. We are a culture that wants to look good, and steroids have become a new if dangerous option to achieve that end.

When I started with steroids, I thought I had found my "magic bullet." Muscles were going to get me respect, and girls. If I could look like someone else, I would no longer be the kid with the stutter. With a set of new muscles, I thought I would be a new person.

Men in particular are vulnerable to the steroid message. We have been increasingly given the message that we need muscles to measure up, to be a man. Some see steroids as the best way to be manly. That makes the allure obvious, and it's not surprising that any warnings against using steroids are usually lost in the fine print. It is easier to put a camera on rippling abs, broad shoulders, and bulging biceps than a spotlight on the unseen price-tag that comes with them.

I consider myself a "steroid survivor." Had I known where my usage would have led me, I would never have taken them. The unfortunate thing is that my story is by no means unique. I consider myself lucky, though, as there are far worse stories out there.

The celebrated steroid bodies run skin deep, and when laid out in a casket they do make for a good-looking corpse. Steroids provide their users with a wonderful mask, but I am here to tell you that the clock is now striking midnight and it's time for the masks to come off.

4

Dr. Jekyll and Mr. Hyde

"O God!" I screamed, and "O God!" again and again;
for there before my eyes – pale and shaken and half
fainting, and groping before him with his hands, like a
man restored from death – there stood Henry Jekyll!

     Robert Louis Stevenson, *Dr. Jekyll and Mr. Hyde*

The confessions of steroid use involving big name athletes are now beginning to emerge. Unfortunately, some
of those admissions are deathbed confessions, or close to it.
In the May 2002 issue of *Sports Illustrated,* former major
league baseball player Ken Caminiti admitted that he had
used steroids for much of his professional career. Two years
later Ken Caminiti was dead. In 1996 Caminiti was the
unanimous selection as the Most Valuable Player of the National League; in the year 2004 he was no longer with us.

Tissue and toxicology tests attributed Caminiti's death to
"Acute intoxication due to the combined effects of cocaine
and opiates." While steroids might not have put the final

nail in Caminiti's coffin, there is no doubt in my mind that they substantially contributed to his passing.

When Caminiti retired from baseball in 2001, his friends reported that he admitted being depressed. Giving up steroids has sent me and many others into a depressive tailspin. More and more studies are showing that this is a vicious circle that can and does kill.

The steroid death toll in professional sports continues to rise every year. Before professional football player Lyle Alzado died of brain cancer, he blamed his long steroid use as the cause of his condition. The medical community never substantiated the link between steroids and Alzado's death, but there is no question but that his behavior suffered as a result of steroid usage. Fellow players described Alzado as having a "split personality." His second wife (he was ultimately married four times) said that because of his steroid use Alzado suffered severe mood swings and would often abuse her (she had to call the police a half dozen times). Alzado knew that his steroid use made him act crazy and do things that he normally wouldn't have, but he couldn't control himself. In a Sports Illustrated article he wrote about his steroid usage, saying, "It was addicting, mentally addicting. I just didn't feel strong unless I was taking something."

The addiction of which Alzado spoke is something that I also experienced. Steroid users begin to feel a psychological need to not only use the drugs, but to up the ante. If you're not using, you feel weak. Think of Martin Sheen playing the role of Captain Willard in the movie *Apocalypse Now*. Sheen's angst at the film's opening reminds me of too many steroid users I have known. One of the first things he says is, "Every minute I stay in this room I get weaker." Steroid users are frightened of being weak, of losing strength. Sometimes they are quite literally frightened to death.

From his grave, Alzado still speaks. Although he achieved success in the National Football League, just before he died Alzado said he wished he had never used steroids. "It wasn't worth it," he wrote. "If you're on steroids or human growth hormone, stop. I should have."

Alzado was 41 when he died. His teammate John Matuszak, another suspected steroid user, died at the age of 38. Alzado said, "A lot of guys on the Raiders asked me about steroids, and I'd help them get what they needed."

Former boxer Bob Hazleton admitted using steroids, and he says they ruined him. Hazleton's legs were amputated as a result of his frequent injections (and subsequent infections). As if the amputations weren't bad enough, Hazleton suffered severe depression and mood swings. He has no doubt that steroids were the root cause of his many problems.

For many years the fraternity of professional athletes has remained tight-lipped concerning the steroid use of their peers, but now that code of silence is beginning to fall. Jose Canseco's book, *Juiced*, implicated many of baseball's most famous players as steroid users. Canseco doesn't seem very repentant about his own use, though, and judging from his words it appears he doesn't think that he experienced any psychological problems from his usage. Perhaps Canseco believes there are other contributing factors that play into his aberrant behavior such as considering suicide and his numerous arrests, including a 1989 citation for a loaded automatic weapon; a 1992 aggravated battery for ramming his then wife's BMW with his own car; a 1997 arrest for striking another wife; and a 2001 brawl in front of a night-club where he and his brother managed to break the nose of one man, and gave a second man 20 stitches.

If Canseco isn't willing to blame anabolic steroids for physical and mental woes, others are. Former NFL lineman Steve Courson developed cardiomyopathy – an enlargement and weakening of his heart – and blamed it on his massive steroid use during his eight years in professional football.

The former Heidi Krieger's story is just as harrowing. In 1986 Krieger became the European women's shot-put champion; steroids were the secret of her success even though she didn't know it at the time. Beginning in 1981 Krieger was given "vitamins" by her coaches. These vitamins turned out to be Oral-Turinabol. After taking the steroids for six months Heidi sprouted muscles – as well as some unwanted side effects. Her voice deepened, and her features became more masculine. Facial hair began to appear. Krieger was at a loss for what was happening to her. Still, while her personal life was miserable, her athletic success was considerable. She was bigger and stronger than she had ever been, and it showed in her performances. Krieger kept pushing her ever larger body, not knowing she was overwhelming her joints. By 1991 Krieger's athletic career was finished, and she left track and field in great pain with debilitating knee, hip, and back problems. The mental toll was even greater.

Krieger was depressed and suicidal. For years she had heard taunts that she was more man than woman. Belatedly she began to realize what the East German sports doctors had done to her. Accepting the changes to her body was difficult; almost as hard was realizing that her athletic performances were a fraud. For a time, suicide seemed to be her only option, but Krieger chose another route: Heidi Krieger became Andreas Krieger. A woman became a man. Krieger, in a *New York Times* interview, insisted that the East German sports machine that foisted steroids, "Killed Heidi."

Andreas Krieger has tried to make peace with his new sex and life. What makes him angry to this day is his belief that he had no choice but to do what he did. Steroids made the decision for Heidi's sex change.

The 2005 Congressional inquiry on steroid use in sports was by no means the first time this nation's government has put the spotlight on steroids. Back in 1989 the Senate Judiciary Committee was looking into steroid use. Sprinter Diane Williams appeared before the committee and confessed her steroid use. Among her revelations: while using steroids she had stopped menstruating; her features had taken on a more masculine appearance; she had sprouted facial hair, and her clitoris had grown to "embarrassing proportions." At the time Williams said, "I am greatly concerned I will ever be able to bear a normal child."

In both professional and amateur sports the trail of steroids can be seen in an increasing number of "smoking gun" cases. Men and women who should be in the prime of their lives are suffering strokes, heart disease, and kidney ailments at a rate far exceeding the norm. The early deaths of still young former (and in some cases current) professional athletes invariably have resulted in speculation upon steroid use.

In one arena where steroid usage is said to be rampant – professional wrestling – the death toll has been astronomical. *USA Today* did an investigation of wrestling deaths in 2004 and discovered that since 1997 nearly 1000 men ages 45 years and younger have worked on the professional wrestling circuit. In that time at least 65 have died, 25 from heart attacks or related illnesses. Statistics tell a damning story: wrestlers have death rates about seven times higher than average, and are 12 times more likely to die from heart disease than are Americans age 25 to 44. Could that just be a coincidence? "If you did not test positive for steroids," joked former wrestler Bruno Sammartino, "you were fired." Sammartino's observation was believed to have more than a grain of truth in it. Wrestling icons Hulk Hogan and Jesse Ventura both admitted to personal steroid use, as well as widespread usage in the sport.

As might be expected, some well known bodybuilders have died at very young ages, and there has been a much higher than average incidence of kidney transplants and heart surgery suffered by individuals in that field. Because of their disproportionate use of steroids, bodybuilders have succumbed more to "the darker side" – so-called "roid rages" – that have resulted in violent behavior and murder.

Among the "murderer's row" are Bertil Fox, a former Mr. Universe convicted of murdering his girlfriend and her mother; John Riccardi, who is now awaiting execution for a double homicide; David Bieber, convicted of killing a London policeman (and suspected of hiring a hit man that killed fellow bodybuilder Markus Mueller); and Gordon Kimbrough, who murdered his fiancée. These cases have been true tabloid fodder, involving such elements as love triangles, stalking, affairs, jealous rages, steroid dealing, and burglary. The common denominator seems to be steroid usage. Bieber's father said, "Once he got into bodybuilding he got into steroids, and that was the beginning of the end. His body and personality changed." As for Kimbrough, one relative said he was, "Meek and shy when not on steroids, and short-tempered and violent when he was using them." At his trial Kimbrough said his long time use of anabolic steroids caused him to fly into an uncontrollable rage during which time he stabbed and strangled his fiancée (a woman with whom he partnered in pair bodybuilding competition).

It is not only male bodybuilders who have committed homicides: Sally McNeil, a well known female bodybuilder, was convicted of the second degree murder of her bodybuilder husband Ray (Mr. California, 1995). Sally shot her husband on Valentine's Day in 1995. Their final fight revolved around the cost of some chicken that Ray was cooking when he was shot.

Is it even conceivable that murder could be committed over the price of chicken?

At her trial Sally said she was a battered wife, and claimed that she killed her husband because she was afraid for her life. The attractive blond former Marine (Sally was a sergeant) was well known in bodybuilding and fitness circles. Now she languishes in Valley State Prison for Women. Both McNeil and her husband were steroid users. Whether that played into his death is unknown; what is known is that steroid users have a propensity to be set off by seemingly trivial offenses.

During my years of abusing steroids my own behavior suffered as a result of my usage. I did things that even now make me cringe to think about. I am only grateful that I never did any permanent harm to anyone, maybe with the exception of myself.

Twice during my college years I participated in the rite of passage known as "spring break." In both years my steroid use ruined the experience. It doesn't help that I mixed alcohol with steroids. I might as well have been mixing gasoline and fire. The steroids made me feel strong and invincible, as well as edgy. Along with giving me bigger shoulders, steroids put a huge chip on top of them. When I drank, that chip became ever more pronounced.

On my first spring break getaway I was walking down the road when a car passed by filled with teens. One of the guys in the car yelled something to me, and I immediately took umbrage. It wasn't as if he said anything too terrible; I was just looking for an excuse to be macho. Because of a traffic light the car was forced to come to a stop, and I took that opportunity to swagger over to it and confront the loudmouth. As I drew near, the front passenger window closed. From inside the car I could see faces looking at me. No one was sticking out their tongues or anything, but it enraged me that they looked so smug behind the glass. I told myself I couldn't let a perceived insult go unpunished. With my open hand I slapped the window, and the glass shattered everywhere. For a moment I stood in a state of shock. I hadn't even thought about how hard I was hitting the glass. With 'roid rage you just react, and that's what I did. I think I was half hoping for a fight; I never imagined the glass would go flying around the car. In a panic, I fled, afraid that I would be arrested for what I had done. With my paranoia fueled, I spent the rest of that spring break in my motel room. The entire time I was fearful that at any moment the police would come knocking at the door to take me away.

When I went to Florida the following year, you would think I might have smartened up some, but that was anything but the case. The longer I took steroids, the more impaired my judgment became.

I was at a club with Jeremy, my friend from college, when I saw a woman who caught my eye. We talked for a time and I began to think I had made a love connection. She attended a college not far from Amherst, and we talked about getting together not only in Florida, but back in Massachusetts. We went our separate ways, but with the understanding that we would hook up later that night. About an hour later I saw this woman talking with another guy – my friend Jeremy. It made no sense, but I was immediately consumed with rage. How dare my friend try and make time with my woman?

I stormed over to Jeremy, a skinny guy who was always quick to tell everyone that he was "a lover, not a fighter." There was no explaining how I felt. I shouted to Jeremy, "I am going to kill you." At that moment, as impossible as it is to believe, I meant every word of what I was saying. The alcohol and steroids had erased every vestige of any common sense I might have had.

Luckily, as I charged at Jeremy, I slipped. Later, Jeremy would claim that he threw a "Muhammad Ali" haymaker at my face. Whether it was the fall or Jeremy's phantom punch, my face landed on the edge of a barstool and shattered my nose. I bled everywhere, and had to be taken to the hospital. In the days that followed my Frankenstein appearance only worsened. I had two enormous black eyes that were set off by all the gauze around my nose. Before appearing in front of my parents, I had a friend call and warn them about what I looked like. Even with the warning, they were shocked by my appearance. Naturally, I had some story concocted about my injury which had nothing to do with steroids or alcohol.

Whenever I look into a mirror even to this day, I have my broken nose as a reminder of my spring break experience. Still, it is a small price that I paid, especially when compared to the consequences suffered by other steroid users.

Jamie Fuller was a novice bodybuilder and only fourteen years old when he started using steroids. Friends and family noticed an immediate change in him. The formerly mild-mannered boy began to act out. Like so many who use steroids, Jamie began to exhibit a Jekyll/Hyde type of personality.

Robert Louis Stevenson wrote *The Strange Case of Dr. Jekyll and Mr. Hyde* in 1885, long before any scientist conceived of anabolic steroids. For many steroid users, though, the fictional account could be the story of their lives. Dr.

Jekyll was a good man who concocted a drug that, in his words, "Shook the doors of the prison-house of my disposition." When Dr. Jekyll drank down this potion, "My virtue slumbered; my evil, kept awake by ambition, was alert and swift to seize the occasion, and the thing that was projected was Edward Hyde."

Henry Jekyll waged war with Edward Hyde for his body and soul. Ultimately Jekyll lost. He could not control Hyde, who committed acts of mayhem and murder with abandon. In the words of Dr. Jekyll, "I had lost my identity beyond redemption." Evil in the form of Hyde proves stronger than good; in the end Jekyll vanishes and only Hyde remains.

When I used steroids, my story was the same as Jekyll's. Jamie Fuller also lost his way, with tragic results. His modern day Jekyll/Hyde story was the basis for the 1996 made for TV movie *No One Would Tell*. The then 16-year-old murdered his 14-year-old girlfriend Amy Carnivale. Fuller claimed he couldn't control his aggression, which was fueled by steroids and alcohol. His rage was set off when he heard that his girlfriend went to a nearby town with another boy. Fuller exacted his revenge later that day. After drinking several beers he grabbed a kitchen knife, lured Amy into the woods, and stabbed her over and over again.

Jamie Fuller was sentenced to life in prison without the possibility of parole. Amy Carnivale wasn't as lucky. Two lives were lost. I have no doubt but that steroids were responsible for that double tragedy. Prior to Fuller's murderous rage, he had taken large doses of testosterone as well as an anabolic steroid in pill form. Fuller's defense team tried to portray his steroid use as a mitigating factor in the murder. The jury might have sympathized, but they couldn't excuse what he did. Fuller will spend the rest of his life in prison.

Because of increased steroid use, Mr. Hyde appears to be emerging with an ever greater frequency. Steroids have the terrible power to transform anyone. Unfortunately, these stories are not being played out in novels, but on police blotters. Even cops themselves aren't immune from steroids. Officers in New York, Alabama, Florida, New Jersey, Ohio, Connecticut, North Carolina, Hawaii, Mississippi, Colorado, and Arkansas have been accused, and in a number of cases convicted, of possessing and/or dealing steroids. Law enforcement is finding itself on the other side of the bar because of steroids. A former Georgia police officer received a life sentence in 1995 for murder, and an Oregon jail guard received a 20-year sentence in 1986 for a kidnapping/shooting. Both men claimed that their steroid use transformed them, and that they would not have otherwise committed these heinous crimes. In 2001 the *Charlotte Observer*'s headline was "Officers Dealt Drugs." An investigation revealed that in Davidson County, North Carolina, law enforcement was not only using steroids, but dealing steroids and street drugs to pay for their "muscle habits." Four police officers were ultimately convicted. New Jersey had a similar case where an officer was arrested for using and selling steroids; in New York a number of cases are now going to trial for officers involved with the "possession, sale, and distribution of controlled dangerous substances, including cocaine and anabolic steroids." Police are often called upon to aggressively respond to situations. Do we want our police officers using anabolic steroids? Could some cases of police brutality be examples of Mr. Hyde coming out?

I almost became Mr. Hyde permanently. For a time I couldn't recognize myself. I deceived and lied and acted violent, and I had no conscience regarding my actions. To get money for steroids, I told my father a string of lies, making up tales such as my car needing a new automatic transmission, or citing nonexistent school fees. Whenever I was home I would regularly rifle my mother's purse. On a number of occasions I made copies of steroid prescriptions given to me by doctors. Lying, stealing, forging – none of that seemed immoral to me. I was just getting money, or finding a means, to obtain something that I thought was necessary.

One time I was at a club with a fellow steroid user everyone called Wig, the kind of guy my mother used to warn me about hanging around with. Wig liked to push people's buttons. He was a bully, just the type of mean kid I hated while growing up. With my new persona, though, I tried to emulate his behavior, so when Wig acted tough to cops outside the club I followed suit. When a policeman shoved Wig, I said, "What the f*** are you doing?"

My big mouth was rewarded with a blow from a police baton to the back of my head. You would think that would have gotten my attention, but when you are Mr. Hyde everything is just water off a duck's back. Wig and I were taken to a holding cell, and the next morning I remember waking up covered in human waste and vomit. The toilets had overflowed and I had picked a spot to camp out between them and the drain. That should have been a reality check, but I hadn't bottomed out yet and I wasn't willing to admit I had a problem.

How could things be wrong? I was big and strong. Even the vomit and effluent couldn't touch me.

Admittedly, most of us do dumb things during our lives. In my own personal equation I had other demons besides steroids, including drug and alcohol use, my youth and inexperience, and self-esteem problems. Still, I was a very different person before and after steroids. Those were my Mr. Hyde years. I did things that were not me. I am mild mannered. Give me Clark Kent any day over a crazed Superman.

Eighteen months after I stopped using steroids my friend Steve dragged me out to a local bar. It didn't take me long before I grew disgusted at what was going on around me. "I can't believe the way these people are behaving," I said.

Steve gave me a look, and then laughed and shook his head. "When you were using steroids," he said, "you would have been the most obnoxious person in here."

It was my turn to give him the funny look. "Really?" I asked.

"That's why I didn't go out with you for a time," said Steve. "You were scary."

Being called "scary" by a friend I'd known since I was a kid wasn't easy to hear, but it was the truth.

For a time I was scary. I wasn't even me.

5

The Hidden Epidemic

We tell ourselves that pestilence is a mere bogy of the mind, a bad dream that will pass away. But it doesn't always pass away and, from one bad dream to another, it is men who pass away.

      ∞ Albert Camus, *The Plague*

When you lead a double-life, you are always afraid of being found out. I took pains to keep my steroid use hidden from my parents. They thought my newfound muscles were the result of all the time I spent at the gym, as well as the various supplements and powders that I always seemed to be taking. Little did they realize that some of those pills I called "vitamins" were actually oral steroids.

The façade to my life of deceit began to crack, though, the summer of my junior year of college. I had a summer job at the Department of Public Works, and I was sitting at my desk when I received a panicked phone call from my mother. It was difficult making sense of her histrionic words, but one word came through loud and clear: needle. She had evidently found one of my syringes.

I rushed home. Since using steroids, I had become a much better liar than I ever could have imagined, and naturally I was ready to give her an Academy Award winning performance.

My mother was waiting for me at the front door, and started in on me as I made my way up the pathway. "Are you using heroin? Are you a junkie?"

"Mom," I told her, offering her a big smile. "You've got it all wrong."

She waved the syringe in her hand as if to say, "How could this be wrong?"

I didn't stop smiling, even though inwardly I was cursing myself for having been careless with my needles. I had slipped up. Until that mistake I had always cleaned up after my usage and secreted everything away. While my mother brandished the syringe, I was doing some waving of my own, showing her a prescription form. By this time we were in the house.

"I am not a junkie, Mom," I told her. "I was given a prescription from a doctor."

"What for?" she asked.

"For steroids," I said, "only steroids."

She still looked doubtful, so I said, "I'll go show you."

I went up to my room and returned with a vial. "See," I said, showing her the vial, and then repeated, "It's only steroids."

It's only steroids. As a parent I can tell you that if I heard those words from one of my two boys I would be as concerned as if my child had announced, "Don't worry, it's only heroin."

I made a big show of throwing out the syringe and vial in front of my mother, all the while offering up some patter about how the doctor had made a big point of insisting that I take an injection of steroids to help ease the pain in some sore muscles. I told her that I didn't think the steroids had really worked, though, and had decided I was done with them. My mother appeared mollified. Luckily, she didn't know anything about steroids, and what I was saying must have sounded reasonable. Besides, my tossing out the vial and syringe clearly demonstrated that I didn't have a problem. What she didn't know was that I had a secret stash in my closet with dozens more vials and needles.

It was also a good thing she didn't look closely at the prescription, or she might have wondered why a vet was prescribing a drug to a human. In my hunt for bigger and better steroids I had found a veterinarian willing to write me a scrip for equipoise, a steroid prescribed for horses. As if that wasn't bad enough, I had made copies of the prescription. I didn't even have horse sense. I was a drug abuser with an illegal prescription covering up his habit by lying.

I wish my mother hadn't trusted me. I wish she had challenged me. I wish she had taken note of all the warning signs my body and behavior were giving off, and had pulled me up short.

According to the U.S. Center of Disease Control, up to 6% of high school students have tried, or are using, steroids. Even if that figure is wildly exaggerated – even if it's only half of that number – we are still talking about an incredible number of young people using steroids.

Teens typically use steroids to get buff or to try and get an athletic edge. What they don't take into account is the Pandora's Box that they open when using steroids. Anyone who uses, or is considering using steroids, needs to take into account the potential hazards that come with the drugs, including:

+ Severe acne (especially on the back and chest)
+ Hair loss
+ Infertility
+ Liver disease, including tumors and cancer
+ Aggressive behavior
+ Testicular atrophy
+ Jaundice
+ Psychological addiction
+ Depression
+ Insomnia
+ Arteriosclerosis (thickening and hardening of arterial walls that interferes with blood circulation)
+ Heart disease – steroid usage elevates the cholesterol and triglyceride levels, putting additional pressure on the heart. Steroids also lower the "good" cholesterol (HDL – high density lipoprotein), and raise the "bad" cholesterol (LDL – low density lipoprotein) which can lead to numerous health problems

* Permanent stunting of growth (premature closing of the epiphysial cartilage which can decrease normal height which would otherwise have been achieved – the earlier steroid use begins, the more inches can be lost)
* Feminization of males including breast swelling (gynecomastia – also known by steroid users as "bitch tits") and fatty deposits
* Skin changes that include stretch marks and skin fissures (females are especially susceptible)
* Water retention (electrolyte imbalances and edema);
* Gastrointestinal symptoms (including diarrhea, nausea, and vomiting)
* High blood pressure
* Kidney damage – kidneys are the filters for the human body, and steroid use puts them under a great deal more strain
* The danger from shared needles and possible exposure to such diseases as HIV, hepatitis and bacterial infections
* Virilization (becoming more masculine) of females, with such symptoms as excessive face and body hair, changes in vocalization (some women experience a deepening of the voice which is irreversible), suppression of menses; decreased breast size; and enlargement of the clitoris
* The potential of steroids being a so-called "gateway" drug
* Wear and tear of tendons and ligaments (steroid usage allows individuals to train harder and exceed the

normal limitations of the body, often resulting in "break-downs")

✦ The health dangers associated with counterfeit or black market steroids made by "cowboy chemists" that have resulted in a host of ailments.

It is hard to believe that given all the health risks (over 70 documented physical and psychological side effects according to an article in the *Journal of Addictive Disorders*) associated with steroids that they continue to grow in popularity. I am afraid that either the message of their dangers isn't getting out, or maybe it's just that the other "message" is so much more prevalent that it's hard to refute. When people look at the hard, muscled bodies presented by smiling, oversized human beings, they see a tempting portrait. Users and potential users are seduced by this picture of health and vitality. The picture doesn't show the strain on the arteries, the wear and tear on the heart, or the pinball effect on the psyche.

In the February 2003 issue of the *Journal of Clinical Psychiatry*, yet another warning flag was raised involving use the usage of anabolic-androgenic steroids (AAS). The authors noted that AAS was frequently not even screened for in drug and alcohol treatment centers, prompting them to conduct a study to see if it might represent "an under-recognized source of morbidity."

In a one year study conducted at McLean Hospital in Massachusetts, preliminary data suggested that "AAS use may have served as a 'gateway' to opioid dependence for these individuals." The authors also speculated that AAS and opioids might stimulate "similar reward pathways in the brain."

While the research is still preliminary, my own personal experience tells me that the doctors are just connecting with the tip of the iceberg. Before I started using steroids I had experimented with alcohol and cannabis, but my use was moderate. The deeper I got into steroid use, the easier it was for me to justify using other drugs. Part of it, I think, was the idea that I was now invincible. I looked strong, so I must be strong, or so I told myself. There was also an element to my thinking that since I was already taking steroids, I didn't see the harm in escalating my behavior. Further, my mind was in a state of flux. I used alcohol and drugs to try and self-medicate the edges of my steroid use. By taking testosterone I seemed to find numerous reasons to abuse any number of other substances.

To show how warped my thinking was, on one occasion I was walking down the sidewalk when a car of kids my own age pulled up to alongside of me. We exchanged friendly nods and then one of them said, "Hey, do you want a good buzz?" I said, "Sure," and he tossed me a baggie with a few pills in it. As the car drove off I did the unthinkable – I swallowed the pills. The way I looked at it, I was already taking pills, and injecting myself, so why not take something else? I am just lucky those pills weren't poison. The doctors might not be able to say it definitively, but I can: if I hadn't been using steroids, I never would have acted that way.

As for the link between opioids and steroids, we're seeing more and more air pollution from that smoking gun. I think of Ken Caminiti's death, and how the autopsy revealed cocaine and opiates in his system. It is time for drug treatment centers to add a new screening test for users; they need to start checking for steroids.

Because society has not yet raised enough red flags over steroid use, the burden for this scrutiny has to fall on parents and loved ones. At the time I abused steroids they were an "under the radar" drug; my parents didn't even know what they were. Public awareness about steroids has grown, but judging from their increased popularity, teens and adults have not yet come to the realization that using them means playing Russian roulette.

To protect their children from the dangers of steroids, parents need to be vigilant. For their own good, no child should be able to get away with what I did. It was wrong of me to pretend insouciance about my drug habit and blithely proclaim, "It's only steroids."

Steroid use *is* the hidden epidemic. Somehow the war on drugs has missed this target. But parents can't afford to turn a blind eye. Among the warning signs parents should be looking for in a child who might be using steroids are:

+ A rapid increase in the musculature of your child
+ Your child's preoccupation or obsession with "getting big"
+ An outbreak of acne (predominately on chest and back) far and above the usual

+ Pronounced mood swings (a tough diagnosis to be sure in volatile teenagers, but look for mercurial Jekyll/ Hyde changes)
+ The presence of muscle magazines (look for the usual smiling steroid figures on the cover). You might have noticed these magazines at the checkout counter of your local pharmacy or supermarket. There's an old axiom: if it's too good to be true, beware. Those bodies are too good to be true
+ The presence of pills, powders, ointments, and liquids that advertise such things as promoting muscle development, or human growth boosters, or testosterone enhancement. Often these are a "smokescreen" for steroid use
+ Vials and pills and syringes – it is up to you to read the labels. I told my parents that the oral steroids I was taking were vitamins. Watch out for the following pills: Anadrol (oxymetholone – sold by the names Oxydrol and Androlic among others); Oxandrin (oxandrolone – most commonly sold as Oxanabol); Dianabol (methandrostenolone – available in such names as Methabol, Anabol, Danabol); Winstrol (stanozolol – marketed as Stanabol and Stanol); tamoxifen; clenbuterol; clomifen citrate (Clomid); masterolone (marketed as Proviron).
+ Anything in a vial is suspect (if it is in a vial, it is usually vile). The brand names are many and varied, but look for the following substances: stanazalol; nandrolone decanoate; dromastolone dipropionate; nandrolone phenilpropionate; chlordehydromethyltestosterone; testosterone

propionate; testosterone enathate; testosterone cipionate; trenbolone acetate; trenbolone hexahydrobencylcarbonate; and boldenone undecylenate.

Despite all those misleading advertisements which claim you can lose 10 pounds of fat and put on 10 pounds of muscle in just a few days, it doesn't happen that way. The human body doesn't change overnight. When not using steroids, professional athletes are hard-pressed to put on 10 pounds of muscle in a year, even with rigorous workouts. If your child suddenly sprouts muscles, it is your job to be suspicious. Don't be surprised if your teen credits those muscles to his or her pumping iron and taking protein shakes and supplements. Speaking from experience, I can tell you that those pills and shakes are all but worthless. Invariably, the spokesperson for those kinds of products is a steroid abuser. The fact is that those supplements will not pack on the pounds and muscles as the manufacturers claim. Steroids will do that. They might also cause you to die or go crazy getting those muscles, but that's not something you are ever likely to hear coming out of the mouth of Mr. Big Deltoids.

What should a parent do if they discover that their child is using steroids? One of the first priorities is to open up a dialogue with your child and start discussing this risky behavior. One of my favorite sayings is, "There is nothing uglier than truth when it is not on your side." Truth is a great antidote to combating steroid usage.

From the onset I would impress upon the child that what they are doing is both illegal and harmful. The Anabolic

Steroid Control Act of 1990, and as amended by The Anabolic Steroid Control Act of 2004 (which amended the definition of steroids to include human growth hormones and other performance enhancing drugs), placed steroids on Schedule III of the Controlled Substances Act. If you take a steroid, in the eyes of the law it's the same thing as popping an amphetamine or Quaalude. Possession of steroids is a federal offense and can result in jail time of up to one year in prison along with a fine up to a thousand dollars. If you manufacture or distribute steroids, the penalties are much more severe. It is common for many steroid users to sell or distribute their drugs. Doing a "favor" for another user can now result in a jail sentence.

Expect your child to be defensive. When you start explaining about health risks associated with steroids, you are sure to hear, "I don't know anybody who has had those kinds of problems." It is entirely possible they'll be telling the truth. You will have to explain that sometimes the effects are not immediate, and sometimes they can't be seen. Tell them that steroids are like cigarettes; often they debilitate over time.

You also have to try and impress upon them what I think of as "the X Factor." Every day more evidence comes forward showing the detrimental effects of steroids. It's only recently that steroids have been linked with depression, just as there have only been preliminary studies on steroids being a possible "gateway" drug. Before the mid-nineties, though, no one was talking about 'roid rage. And before that no one had any idea about the potential for kidney damage and arteriosclerosis due to steroid usage.

Your child will tell you that steroids work, and he'll be right. They do work, but it's one of those cases of their working too well. Your child might not want to hear about heart disease or liver tumors or hardening of the arteries. You will hear about the strength gains, and the "incredible" workouts. Your response should be, "At what cost?" The human body is designed for certain maximum levels. Those who abuse steroids can, and do, spend more time at the gym or on the playing field and are able to push themselves harder and longer. Sooner, rather than later, though, the human body rebels; joints tear and ligaments rip. It isn't surprising that sports medicine has seen an epidemic of career ending injuries in the past decade. Steroids have given athletes a false platform upon which to perform; when that platform collapses, too often it is game, set, and match. This trend of serious injuries extends from high schools to the professional levels. Sports doctors say they are seeing a huge increase in tendon and muscle ruptures. That isn't a coincidence. When bodies get pushed too hard, they snap even harder.

Student athletes are under enormous pressure to perform and that makes steroids tempting. Non-athletes feel their own pressures; everyone wants to look "buff" and fit. Parents should also tell their children that steroids are cheating. In simple terms of right and wrong, they are wrong, and you don't want your child to be a cheater. If your son or daughter is looking for an athletic advantage, tell them that you don't believe in winning at all costs and neither should they. Stress to them that the muscles they think they are getting are artificial and temporary, and if they want the real thing then they are going to have to work for it. Talk to your child and make sure his or her self-esteem is not dependent on body image. This will probably be another case where your child thinks you are old-fashioned and out of it; when your child grows up he will see how wise you were (but don't expect to get thanked any time soon).

It is possible your child has body dysmorphia, with a resulting skewed view on what his/her body really looks like. Harrison Pope established a formula to calculate what he called the "fat-free mass index" (FFMI). Based on those calculations, the upper limits of musculature and build can be defined by their scoring system. The researchers found that a drug-free individual could be muscular, but in a proportional and natural way. Unfortunately, these days we see so many images of bodies accomplished through steroids that we don't realize them for what they are – fakes. Teens need to have a realistic idea of what is normal body image and what is abnormal.

When confronting a child's usage of steroids, the natural reaction for any concerned parent is to ban steroids from the household. That prohibition won't work, though, unless your child realizes it is in his own best interest to quit. Going off steroids is something that can be fraught with problems. Consult with a doctor. Going "cold turkey" can have tragic consequences. If you get steroids out of your house, be aware that your child might seek out steroids through friends and find a way to try and hide further usage from you. Don't be afraid of being the "bad guy." Your child might not understand the serious consequences involved with steroid usage. If you suspect continued use of steroids, take your son or daughter to a physician and have them tested.

I would also strongly encourage you to get your child into counseling. Most males will resist this, and will no doubt insist that it's unnecessary. These are the same males who might suffer severe depression in silence, not doing anything about it. Unfortunately their ultimate solution might be suicide. Without being overly dramatic, parents need to be on a "suicide watch" for a child who is using steroids or has recently stopped. Coming down from steroids can be a perilous time, especially for young people. They need to understand what is happening to them. Because they have tinkered with their body chemistry, stopping steroid usage might result in considerable physical and mental shocks to the system.

When young men act rambunctious, people often roll their eyes and say, "Too much testosterone." Imagine, then, too much testosterone for months and years at a time. Your child needs to know that's what they wreaked upon their system, and that sometimes body and mind take time to find their way back to normal.

Take it from me; it will be one of the most important journeys they ever undertake.

The Emperor's New Clothes

So off went the Emperor in procession under his splen-did canopy. Everyone in the streets and windows said, "Oh, how fine are the Emperor's new clothes! Don't they fit him to perfection? And look at that long train!" Nobody would confess that he couldn't see anything, for that would prove him either unfit for his position, or a fool. No costume the Emperor had worn before was ever such a complete success.

"But he hasn't got anything on," a little child said.

     ✑ Hans Christian Andersen, *The Emperor's New Clothes*

One of my primary motivations for writing this book is that I am a father of two young boys, and though I can't hope to protect my children from all the evils in the world, I am trying to give them the kind of upbringing that will allow them to make good choices in their lives as to what is right and what is wrong. All parents want the best for their children. In a world of sound bites and images, though, it is easy for children to lose their way. As a concerned parent, I want my children to be able to look long and hard at both the overt and subliminal messages that are constantly being thrown at them. I hope my children will be able to look at the emperor's new clothes and say to a deluded crowd around them, "But he hasn't got anything on."

It's hard to separate the chaff from the wheat, especially when the chaff is being pushed on us all the time. No one is immune from all the messages being thrown at us, but we can try and give our kids a "common sense" vaccine that will allow them to scrutinize the false promise of anabolic steroids, as well as a host of other empty seductions.

Going against popular culture isn't easy. Teens know what a steroid body looks like. If you tell them that what they are seeing is the emperor without any clothes, they'll probably think you are crazy. How can rippling muscles, bulging biceps, and massive shoulders not be viewed as something substantial and desirable? Tell them the fable; tell them the facts; put a focus on the huge shadow that lurks behind the steroid body. It's that shadow they need to see more than the inflated body.

Because of my little boys I am reacquainting myself with a lot of fables and folktales. The great thing about these stories is their message resonates with people of all ages. You might remember in *The Emperor's New Clothes* that two con men pose as tailors. They pantomime that they are weaving the finest and most luxurious of fabrics. Naturally, they need all sorts of money for their golden thread. When the emperor sends his trusted advisers to check on how their progress is proceeding, the "tailors" continue their show of making the outfit. No one is willing to say they can't see the fabric; they are afraid that by doing so they'll look feeble and dumb and certainly not worthy of their office. If the emperor sees the fabric, they reason, why then it must exist. In the end all the nobles, the court, and the people agree on what beautiful clothes the emperor has. When the emperor goes out in public to show off his finery, the crowd makes much to do about their ruler's wonderful, if nonexistent, clothes. Finally it is left to a child to say the obvious.

Who are the new con men selling us the emperor's clothes? To get that answer, one need only follow the money. That is the reason these hoaxes are being perpetrated. The trail leads in many directions: diet supplements; pills; magazines; videogames; advertising; gyms; fitness equipment; and movie hype, to name but a few. I make my living helping people improve their fitness, but I don't condone the false body images being pushed on us and our children.

While I admire Arnold Schwarzenegger's long-time involvement with Special Olympics and the Inner-City Games, and applaud the fact that he has used his celebrity status to help the disadvantaged, as well as to try and offer an alternative to gangs, drugs, and violence, I am still uncomfortable with him being touted as a role model for fitness. To my thinking, steroids are the opposite of fitness. In his February 27, 2005 interview on *This Week with George Stephanopoulos*, Schwarzenegger admitted to using steroids during his years as a bodybuilding champion (he was the seven-time Mr. Olympia) and said, "I have no regrets about it." Schwarzenegger also said, "At that time it was something new that came on the market and we went to the doctor and did it under doctors' supervision."

When Schwarzenegger was appointed Chairman to the President's Council on Physical Fitness from 1990 to 1993, I thought the wrong message was being sent to American youths. The Council on Physical Fitness is supposed to "promote, encourage, and motivate Americans of all ages to become physically active and participate in sports." Choosing my all-time poster boy of steroids is like putting the emperor's clothes on display. To this day one of the slang terms for steroids is "Arnolds" (steroids also go by the slang of 'roids, juice, hype, and pump), and one of the biggest professional bodybuilding contests in this country, and the world, is the "Arnold Classic." The Arnold Classic is definitely not one of the so-called "natural" bodybuilding competitions. Does Governor Schwarzenegger think that reflects well upon him?

To his credit, Schwarzenegger is now urging bodybuilding officials to crack down on steroid use, and at the 2005 Arnold Classic he came out and said, "We have to step up the testing procedures and find other ways to be more aggressive with it."

The fact remains, though, that Arnold Schwarzenegger *is* the current executive editor of *Flex* and *Muscle and Fitness* magazines. Judging by the pictorials (or is that pec-torials?) displayed in those magazines, it seems to me that Arnold can't say one thing and then tacitly condone the opposite with his silence. Maybe it's just me, but I can't watch *Kindergarten Cop* without feeling very uneasy.

Being a celebrity doesn't mean you're infallible. I have never been very politically active, but the 2005 Congressional hearings looking into steroid usage in professional baseball awakened a newfound fervor in me. One congressman was quoted as saying that his staff was very excited about all the athletes that would be appearing to testify, and he said that they wanted him to ask for autographs. That prompted me to make a call his office to say, "You should be asking tough questions, not for autographs." I also spent considerable time talking to an aide of another congressman discussing points that I believed needed to be addressed. Famous athletes can't be given a free pass for doing the wrong thing, and neither should politicians.

There are alternatives to the parade of steroid bodies known as professional bodybuilding competitions, but these so-called drug free bodybuilding contests have not proved nearly as popular as the anabolic steroid shows. People have come to expect a freak show, but maybe with these competitions there should be the kind of warning that goes on all cigarette packaging. Instead of masking as fitness proponents, we might be better served to label these bodybuilders as what they are – drug abusers and felons. It would be nice at the start of these spectacles for children to hear a warning come over the intercom stating, "Because many of these bodybuilders regularly put dangerous levels of Schedule III drugs into their bodies as stipulated by the Controlled

Substances Act, they violate the laws of this land, and might suffer the following ailments . . ."

I would also love to see those same warnings plastered in muscle magazines. My alternative publication might look more like a rogue's gallery. I could display the oiled and tanned and hugely muscular body of the man who killed his wife, and put the warning: Steroid use might result in homicide. Or I could put on a display over the pecs of the huge bodybuilder who had a heart attack: Steroid use can lead to heart disease. There are no shortage of bodybuilders, and body parts, that I could label. Such a magazine might counter the propaganda put out by the anabolic steroid lobby.

There needs to be an alternative message, and right now there really isn't one. I consider myself a spiritual, if not religious, man. When I was younger I wish I had paid more attention to the Second Commandment: Thou shalt not make unto thee any graven images. The world of steroid bodybuilding is an altar to producing false idols. It is no wonder that one of the slang terms for a steroid body is "freaky."

When I gave up steroids I threw away a huge collection of muscle magazines. For a long time I worshipped graven images, until finally I realized that everything I was looking at was a fraud. I suppose I finally came full circle and was able to see with the eyes of a young child. Maybe that's why Andersen's story of *The Emperor's New Clothes* so resonates with me. I became that child looking at the emperor and his new clothes. Still, I had trouble dealing with my body image after readjusting from steroids. Even after emerging from the year that was the black hole of my life, I didn't want to look at my normal body. One day I finally confessed to my father that I hadn't looked into a mirror for a year and a half. He couldn't believe that.

"How do you shave?" he asked.

"I feel around my face," I told him.

He shook his head in disbelief. "Why don't you look in the mirror?"

"I'm not quite ready," I told him.

It wasn't too long after that when I began looking back into mirrors. By then my head was on straight enough that I didn't need to see fake muscles. I had chosen the real world over illusion, and believe it or not, when I did start looking at mirrors again I was happy with what I saw. There were some changes to be sure. I was thinner and my muscles weren't so pronounced. My years of steroid abuse and inflated muscles had left massive stretch marks on my shoulders, but what I saw was the real me. The bloated look that had altered my face and announced me as a steroid user had all but vanished, and my eyes were once again clear. I could see.

Billy Crystal used to do a skit on Saturday Night Live where he would imitate Fernando Lamas and say, "It's not how you feel, it's how you look." And then he would add with smug intonation, "And you look marvelous!" Remembering his imitation still makes me laugh, but behind the comedy is a great deal of reality. When it comes right down to it, the message of steroids is to not worry about the consequences, and not consider what you are doing to yourself. The only thing that matters is how you look.

In several passages in this book I have used the phrase "pay the piper." That expression comes from the children's story, The Pied Piper of Hamelin. You might remember that in the story the Mayor of Hamelin contracted with the Pied Piper to rid his city of rats. The piper played, and the rats followed his music into the harbor where they drowned, but when it came time to settle the payment the mayor reneged on the deal. The piper warned him of dire consequences, but the mayor didn't listen. The rats were gone, the mayor reasoned, so he didn't care about the piper's threats. When the piper played next, his tune drew forth all the children of the town. They ran after the piper, followed him into an opening in the mountain, and were never seen again.

The moral is that you have to pay the piper. When discussing steroids with teens I like to tell the story of the Pied Piper. Steroids are seductive, and it's not hard to see why kids are attracted to them. In most cases they will make you bigger and stronger in a shorter period of time, but parents need to make clear the cost of steroids. If you use them, you will have to pay the piper, and sometimes the cost is very high.

Robert Fulghum took a nice phrase and made a good book out of it: *All I Really Need to Know I Learned in Kindergarten.* If we remind our children of those Golden rules, then they might not be as ready to use steroids. In case you forgot those kindergarten lessons, one of the first rules we learned was to "play fair."

Steroids don't play fair.

Another rule that was stressed was, "Clean up your own mess." With steroids you are at risk of making your own life a mess, as well as the lives of others.

And then there is the rule, "Don't take things that aren't yours." I should have remembered that when I was taking steroids and I found out that the muscles I had weren't really mine. Ben Johnson had his Olympic gold medal taken away when it was discovered he used steroids. There's a name for people who take things that aren't theirs: cheaters.

If you hearken back to what you learned in kindergarten, you know that steroids violate most of the Golden rules you learned. Unfortunately, it seems that many good lessons are forgotten as we get older.

Many boys have dreams of being professional athletes, and it is those dreams that have prompted the steroid use of countless youths. I believe in dreams, but I do like to temper them with reality. If a child you know thinks steroids are a ticket to an athletic scholarship and a career in sports, they need to think again. Ask that child if it is worth chancing a permanent injury or ill health in the hope that taking steroids might yield an athletic edge. A healthy passion for sports will usually get an individual much further than an unhealthy obsession. For the vast majority of teens, hitting the books is a much better way of getting ahead than hitting a ball. Even the very best athletes seldom make it to the professional ranks.

Statistics tell the story. Every year there are about two million American boys that play high school football, basketball, and baseball. Of that number, approximately 70,000 will go on to play those sports in college. The professional ranks dwindle those numbers even more dramatically. Only 2500 professional athletes play the "big three" sports, and a significant number of those come from countries other than America. If you break down the numbers, one in 27 high school players goes on to play in college, and one in 736 will go on to play at the professional level (that translates to 0.14%).

At the height of my steroid use, I was paying hundreds of dollars a month for my drugs. I hate to admit it, but it appears much of my money went to the Russian Mob, as they were smuggling in most of the steroids that were sold on the east coast in the 1980's. Nowadays it is easier than ever to get steroids; there are more varieties of synthetic testosterone available, and production occurs in most parts of the globe because relatively few countries have restrictions upon its manufacture. Getting the drugs into this country has not proved difficult. In a July 13, 2004 speech in front of the U.S. Senate Caucus on International Narcotics Control, Deputy Drug Enforcement Agency Director Joseph T. Rannazzsi said, "Criminal organizations of Russian, Romanian, and Greek nationals are significant traffickers of steroids and are responsible for substantial shipments of steroids entering the United States."

As the U.S. Customs Service writes on its website, "Steroids are like any other illegal drug that threatens the American public – like all illegal narcotics their sale and possession represent critical links in a larger criminal process, one that funds terrorism, death and addiction all around the world."

I don't think that most people like supporting criminal enterprises. We need to get the message out there that every time someone buys steroids, they cross that line.

There are legitimate manufacturers of anabolic steroids throughout the world, but the majority of drugs produced never get used for the purpose that was intended for them. Boldenone undecylenate is a steroid manufactured under a variety of names throughout the world; in Canada it is sold as Equipoise and used on horses; in Colombia it goes by the name of Ganabol and is used for cattle; in Germany it is called Vebonol and is prescribed for dogs. The drug labels often show the animal for which the steroid is intended, and yet these steroids are being used by humans.

When steroids almost killed me I used to tell people that I thought rats were crawling out of my head. I know it sounds crazy, and it was, but I was really having that hallucination. I suppose I was lucky to not be imagining horses, cows, and dogs also crawling out.

7

Beyond Pandora's Box

*Suffering has been stronger than all other teaching and
has taught me to understand what your heart used to
be. I have been bent and broken, but – I hope – into a
better shape.*

∾ Charles Dickens, *Great Expectations*

It is understandable that people are curious about using
anabolic steroids. With a growing percentage of individuals dissatisfied with their body image, it is easy to see why
steroids have an allure. Dieting and exercise isn't easy. In a
busy world, all of us are looking for shortcuts. It is possible
some of you know people who have used steroids who don't
appear to have suffered any consequences. If they reaped
the benefits of looking bigger and better without any harm
coming to them, then why shouldn't you?

In the words of Clint Eastwood's Dirty Harry, "Well, do
you feel lucky punk? Well, do you?" You might be one of the
lucky ones. Maybe there isn't a bullet in the chamber. I like

to tell people, though, that when you take steroids, you open Pandora's Box.

Pandora, for those of you who slept through Greek mythology, was the first woman created by the gods. When Pandora came to earth she was given a box and instructed, warned by the gods and goddesses even, that whatever she did she must not open the box.

What the gods didn't tell Pandora was what was in the box. Being curious, she went back to the box time and again. She shook it, and listened to it, and examined it. And finally one day she decided to peek into the box and just take a quick, little look. She opened the box only a crack, but that was enough. In a flash, all the ills that were to afflict the world flew out. Plague, famine, disease, and heartbreak, to name but a few, escaped the box (stinging her along the way). Pandora shut the lid, but it was too late. Paradise was lost.

Pandora grieved at what she had done. Because of her curiosity, everyone would suffer. Too late, she went to put away the accursed box, and that's when she heard the voice from inside of it. There was still one occupant in the box, and it called for Pandora to let her out. Pandora resisted at first, knowing what her curiosity had wrought, but finally she relented and opened the box. What emerged was a being who called herself Hope, and Hope told her that although Pandora had brought great harm upon humans, she (Hope) would always be there to aid them in their troubles.

There is hope for people who have opened the Pandora's Box of steroids, and I am living proof of that.

When I quit steroids and had my breakdown I found myself seemingly alone in the wilderness. Most of the doctors I saw had no knowledge of anabolic steroids. There were no studies about depression resulting from steroid usage. Medical professionals had no inkling that steroids could be psychologically addictive, and there was next to no literature on the subject for them to consult. Because of that, doctors and shrinks could not understand, let alone treat, my symptoms. Not because I wanted to, but because I had to, I became a human guinea pig. Doctors misdiagnosed my symptoms and prescribed the wrong meds; mental health professionals had no idea why I was so depressed. In order to survive, it became a matter of "physician heal thyself."

I started going to AA and Narcotics Anonymous (NA meetings). To my knowledge there weren't, and still aren't, any Steroids Anonymous meetings, but I found kindred souls at the AA and NA gatherings. There are many of the same components involved in drug, alcohol and steroid abuse, and those meetings allowed me access to support groups. Perhaps one day I will start an SA chapter, but in the interim my advice for steroid abusers is to begin with AA meetings.

At the onset of my going to AA I had some problems with adhering to the twelve-step program. My background wasn't a religious one, and humbling myself to a God that I had rarely prayed to didn't make sense to me. Part of the reason I was attracted to steroids was that I had falsely thought they would make me be powerful enough to not need anyone or anything. Who needs God if you can look like the Incredible Hulk? Bottoming out, though, I came to new realizations.

My Uncle was very religious, and in my despair I asked him to pray for me, and he told me that he was. Talk about lifting weights! I felt a burden taken from me. In time I came to know that there is a God, and the twelve steps started becoming a part of my life.

My life was unmanageable. I did need to be restored to sanity. I turned my life over to God *as I understood Him;* I did my moral inventory; I tried to figure out my wrongs; I asked God to improve my character and remove my short-comings; I tried to make amends to those I harmed, and I'm still trying; I took my own personal inventory, and continue to do so; I try to carry out God's will *as I understand Him;* and I'm trying to carry this message to steroid users. This book is for them, and to prevent others from getting tangled in their web.

Still, AA and NA weren't enough for me. The meetings addressed many of my issues, but I still needed healing in other ways. One doctor prescribed antidepressants for me. I tried them, but they didn't help. In the years since there have been great improvements in psychopharmacology, and per-haps I would have found relief had the antidepressants of today been available to me, but I was forced to look elsewhere.

I tried therapy and hypnotherapy, but neither helped me very much. Therapists, like the doctors, knew very little about anabolic steroids. When I described my issues, they were at a loss as to how to deal with them. Nowadays thera-pists might be more knowledgeable, but I wouldn't count on it. Most medical and mental health professionals are still not very well versed on steroids. The situation is not helped by the fact that most juice-heads are bad patients. Those who are coming off steroids tend to be irritable, depressed, and downright hostile. They have come from an arena of *power*, and hate the idea of debasing themselves. They are ashamed, and angry, and their pride makes them hate the whole process of their perceived humiliation. *Freaks* (and believe it or not, they view that as a positive word) detest having to debase themselves to geeks (an overall view of the non-steroid medical community). Because they are used to taking matters into their own hands, steroid users are reluctant to seek out treatment. For many, suffering in silence is better than appearing weak. They think that "real" men (which they typically believe translates only to those with muscles) don't whine. Coming clean is difficult for them because they have been leading secretive lives from everyone but fellow meatheads.

I can say all these things matter-of-factly not only because I've heard these stories from doctors and mental health professionals, but because I was that suspicious, reluctant, and at times, even hostile patient. How bad was I? I trusted my gym "doctor" Big Bob more than I did medical doctors who had graduated from Harvard University. Big Bob, I could see, was practicing what he was preaching. He knew about steroids firsthand. What did these eggheads really know about juice? With the wisdom of years I now know that Big Bob should have been called Big Boob, but for a long time I was sure his word was the gospel truth.

Crawling out of the desert wasn't easy; mirages haunted me. But luckily I found an oasis or two along the way.

Ironically, what almost destroyed me is what saved me. Exercise proved to be my salvation. The idea of appearing as fit as possible drove me to extremes; becoming truly fit brought me back to sanity.

The doctors and mental health professionals were wise enough to recommend exercise for me, but I was disdainful of their advice. Their idea of exercise was to take a walk, or ride a bicycle, but hearing that nostrum delivered to a man who at one time could bench-press 400 pounds sounded like an insult. I was used to pounding weights; I was used to sweating buckets and making noises and growling while throwing around iron. I knew I needed to exercise, but not the way in which they were suggesting. In desperation I tried returning to the gym, but right away I knew that was a dead end. I wasn't as strong, and the meatheads were all around. To me, they looked like vultures hovering around my body.

What I knew, even if I couldn't explain or articulate at the time, was that my mind and body were detached. Somehow I had to find a way to bridge this schism. Not doing so wasn't an option; I was sick in soul and spirit. Still, I didn't know how to make that connection.

The first glimmer of an answer came to me as I was sitting around my parent's home. For too long I'd been in little more than a "vegetative state," but one day I caught sight of five pound dumbbells, and probably because I was bored more than anything I picked one up. At the gym I was used to working with 100 pound dumbbells; I would have been embarrassed to use five pound dumbbells unless I was working out my pinky. Still, I took that five pound dumbbell and did a bicep curl. I had worked with weights for years, but that small motion made a connection that had always escaped me before. I became mindful of the movement; the motion in my arm connected with my brain, and it felt good and right. My brain was in synch with my arm. At the time I didn't know I had found my "missing link" – I just knew I felt better than I had in some time.

I switched hands and repeated the motion with the dumbbell. My movements were slow and purposeful. Something that easy shouldn't have made me feel so good, but it did. The steroid version of me would have wanted to start throwing around 50 pound dumbbells; the new me just continued with the movement. My body and mind began to reacquaint themselves. Yes, they seemed to be saying, this is what we need. We were once bonded, but that was before the great steroid divorce.

Before, my workouts had always been designed for outward appearance. Now I began to look inwards. It was no longer a matter of how I looked; the more important process was how I felt. All my previous regimens had been based on the external; now I was discovering the internal. It was a whole new world for me, and I knew that I needed to explore it.

Using this body and mind approach, I found a new and better way to do my workouts. I was a product of the "no pain, no gain" school, which made what I was doing seem all the more revolutionary. Instead of using big weights, I used smaller weights; instead of pumping iron fast and hard I became slow and deliberate; instead of beating my chest like a gorilla, I made friends with my body; instead of treating my lungs like bellows, I became very deliberate in my breathing, and mindful of every breath. By concentrating on my breathing, by being mindful of the muscles I was working, by working mind and body in tandem, my workout became a form of meditation. Those who do Yoga or meditate are likely acquainted with the principles of this process, but I didn't have that background. I had always associated workouts with brute force, so I was amazed that doing these exercises was not only making me stronger but providing other windfall benefits as well. My depression began to dissipate; each time I worked out I felt better. Whereas I had always viewed weight-training as a necessary evil to look good, these exercises weren't like that. They were enjoyable, and they massaged a muscle that I had always overlooked: my mind.

Injury and burnout are usually part and parcel with steroid use and weight-training. The human body breaks down when pushed in such unnatural ways. With the method I developed, my body and mind embraced the workout. In fact I stopped even thinking of what I did as a workout; it was just fun. That was hard for me to accept. Could what I was doing really be beneficial if I wasn't experiencing pain? I was skeptical, but I couldn't deny the results. With the passing of every day, I felt physically, mentally, and spiritually stronger. I even gave a name to what I was doing, calling it "Mindful Movements."

I didn't need a gym; I didn't need steroids; I didn't need huge weights. My place of exercise was the living room. My only goal was harmony, but along with peace of mind my muscles began to return. That wasn't a priority, though. My perception of exercise had changed. The ancient Greek ideal was to be sound in mind and sound in body. I had forgotten the mind part. As my union of mind-body fitness worked its wonders on me I was incredibly excited. Like Archimedes, I wanted to yell, "Eureka!" I had found it, and I had found myself.

The "new" me wanted to help others. I began to tell friends (even strangers) about my program. At the time I was an accountant at a bank, but I wasn't nearly as enthusiastic about pushing numbers as I was about pushing Mindful Movements. A friend of mine encouraged me to, in the words of Joseph Campbell, "Follow my bliss." There was no question in my mind that my bliss would help others become whole again as it had for me. The next day I quit my job and started building my dream. I followed my bliss and opened Custom Fitness.

I like to tell people that Custom Fitness is an "anti-gym." One of our philosophies is that we take the work out of workout. It's been my experience that those establishments that call themselves "health clubs" usually are not very healthy. They are for the "meat" and "meets" – meatheads and meet markets. I wanted a facility where you could actually meet yourself, the very person I had gone to such pains to avoid.

Custom Fitness is located in Boston. As health clubs go, it is not typical. We don't sell supplements, protein bars, or pills or powders. We don't have a juice bar. The only liquid we have is spring water or seltzer water; the only food we have is complimentary healthy snacks. There are no meat-heads tossing about iron. In fact our clients exercise in total privacy in separate studios. We don't have pictures of bodybuilders; all we have are a few posters with inspirational quotations (my favorite is General Omar Bradley's: "We need to learn to set our course by the stars, not by every passing ship"). Loud rock music doesn't blare over loud-speakers. Our personal trainers don't run around in cutoffs, or in clinging spandex, but wear professional uniforms instead. Our mirrors are minimal, whereas in steroid gyms "funhouse" mirrors abound. The truth of the matter is that we don't even have a scale. We want to incorporate changes into lives that transcend what mirrors or scales tell.

As gyms go, we are not sexy and don't try to be. We have four private exercise rooms with state of the art equipment for clients to work one-on-one with their trainer. Once people try us, their perception of exercise is changed forever. Clients tell us, "You work miracles." That might be overstating it, but those are words we love to hear.

Word of our unique approach to strengthening mind and body began to circulate around Boston, and that's when doctors and mental health professionals began to refer patients to us. Many of those who come to us are suffering from depression, or emotional difficulties, or a substance abuse problem; most of our clients would never step foot in a mainstream gym. One of my clients was severely injured in a car accident more than twenty years ago; her injury left her with limited mobility. She had tried rehab, other gyms, and different personal trainers, and had found neither comfort nor success. Like so many others, she was turned off by the gym scene. After hearing about my philosophy of mind/body exercise, she relayed the information back her husband and he said, "We can pay for a funeral, or we can pay for this."

I am glad to say they didn't pay for a funeral. That client came to me on the same crutches she had been using for many years. After we worked with her, she lost the crutches (for good) and ended up dancing at her daughter's wedding.

When I modeled the design and philosophy of Custom Fitness, I did so with the idea of making it a health club to help people in need. After giving up steroids, there was no health club for me to go to and heal. I remember my own needs, and how they weren't met; I wanted to build a haven to help those sick in mind, or body, or both.

I would like to think my program is the right antidote for those going through steroid "detox." At the same time I realize that each individual has unique problems and needs. These days some treatment centers have recognized the problems associated with anabolic steroids, and offer recovery programs with a number of therapies including twelve step programs, nutritional guidance, fitness consultations, anger therapy sessions, body dysmorphic disorder treatment, psychopharmacology options, and family therapy. I found my deliverance through exercise; you might need antidepressants, or therapy, or a combination of treatments.

The better answer is prevention, of course. When it comes to steroids, we need to start shouting the line that was always used in westerns, and "cut them off at the pass."

Educating high school students on the dangers of steroid use could very well prevent stories like mine. One promising program currently in use is called ATLAS (Athletes Training & Learning to Avoid Steroids), a curriculum that involves coaches and peer leaders in discussing the dangers of steroids with students and offers those students the better alternatives that can be gained through nutrition and strength training. According to studies, in the high schools utilizing this program new steroid use was reduced by 50 percent. We can't fool ourselves and think that a slogan like "Just Say No" will dissuade teens from taking steroids. Hearing from peers and coaches that taking steroids is not the right choice might very well be the most successful way of tainting their allure.

My advice: don't open Pandora's Box. If you already have, though, hope is out there just waiting to be found.

Oh, Say Can You See?

*People always told me that my natural ability and good
eyesight were the reasons for my success as a hitter.
They never talk about the practice, practice, practice!*

> ✍ Ted Williams (the last hitter in major league
> baseball to bat over .400)

On March 17, 2005 I watched Donald Hooton testifying
before the House Government Reform Committee's hearings
on steroid use in Major League Baseball. The pain I saw on
Hooton's face reminded me of the haunted look on my own
father's face when I was trying to escape the grip of steroids.
Mr. Hooton was not as lucky as my father, though. Just
twenty months prior to his testimony before the committee,
his son Taylor took his own life.

Like too many other teens, Taylor felt the need to "get bigger." He wanted to be a starting pitcher on the varsity baseball team. According to Hooton, Taylor used anabolic
steroids "as a shortcut to reach his objective."

By all accounts Taylor was a good kid. He had a high G.P.A. and was popular. Mr. Hooton is certain that his son's secret use of steroids, in his words, "Played a significant role in causing the severe depression that resulted in his suicide."

Most of the media turned out to see the multimillionaire baseball players paraded out to talk (or, as turned out to be the case, to mostly *not* talk) about steroids in baseball, but the real story was the testimony of Hooton and Denise Garibaldi who spoke for children no longer around to tell their stories.

Rob Garibaldi also dreamed of playing Major League Baseball. Like Taylor Hooton, he also felt the need to get bigger. After he graduated from high school Rob went to Tijuana, Mexico, and purchased steroids. It was the beginning of the end for him. Rob was a good enough player to get a full scholarship to baseball power-house University of Southern California; he even played for USC in the 2000 College World Series. Steroids helped him gain weight and muscle, but they also pushed him over the brink.

Although Mr. and Mrs. Garibaldi confronted Rob about his suspected steroid use, he told them they were mistaken. Firsthand, though, Mrs. Garibaldi said they witnessed his, "Mania, depression, short-term memory loss, uncontrollable rage, delusional and suicidal thinking, and paranoid psychosis." According to Mrs. Garibaldi, "Prior to steroids, Rob never displayed any of these symptoms. When not on steroids or in withdrawal from them, Rob was a sweet and emphatic guy with ambition beyond baseball."

Rather than helping him achieve his dream of playing major league baseball, steroids destroyed that dream. Rob was dismissed by the coaching staff at USC as a "behavior problem." When the 2002 Major League draft occurred Rob was not selected because scouts had decided he was a "head case."

Mr. and Mrs. Garibaldi tried to get Rob the care he needed; he was hospitalized, put on medication, and treated in a residential treatment facility, but steroids already had him in their death grip. Rob committed suicide at the age of 24.

It was only through luck that my life did not end like Taylor Hooton's and Rob Garibaldi's. The loss of these young lives makes me sad – and angry. I watched much of the eleven hours of the televised testimony of the congressional inquiry into steroids, and nothing touched me like the pain of those parents.

Like most members of the House Government Reform Committee, I didn't come away satisfied as to how Major League Baseball is handling the issue of steroids and steroid testing. Massachusetts Representative Stephen Lynch spoke for me when he said, "I have not been reassured one bit by the testimony I have heard today." Lynch went on to add that MLB's testing program, "Has so many loopholes, it is just unbelievable."

Kentucky Senator Jim Bunning knows the ins and outs of the baseball diamond better than most. Before he entered politics he was a Hall of Fame pitcher in the 1950s and 1960s. "What's happening in baseball is not natural," he said to the committee, "and it's not right."

Bunning pointed out the obvious – the huge weight and muscle gains of players, and ballplayers hitting more home runs in their late thirties than they did in their late twenties.

He was incensed at how the game of baseball – America's National Pastime – had been tarnished, and he didn't spare his judgment saying that when it came to players illegally using steroids we should, "Wipe all their records out. Take them away. They don't deserve them."

Even the President of the United States has not been immune from the steroid controversy. In his 2004 State of the Union Address President George W. Bush said, "Unfortunately, some in professional sports are not setting much of an example for our children. The use of performance-enhancing drugs like steroids in baseball, football and other sports is dangerous, and it sends the wrong message: that there are shortcuts to accomplishment and that performance is more important than character. So tonight I call on team owners, union representatives, coaches and players, to take the lead, to send the right signal, to get tough and to get rid of steroids now."

On April 15, 2005, President Bush again spoke out against steroids, saying they have "put a cloud over baseball," and adding that he believed that cloud would linger until confidence was restored to the game's integrity by team owners and players. As for the question of whether asterisks should be attached to the records of players associated with steroids, the president said that "experts and philosophers" would have to make that decision.

Despite the president's assertions, there is little to indicate that professional sports are motivated to change the current status quo when it comes to steroids. Cynics suggest that sports like baseball benefit from the spectacle of big bodies hitting towering home runs, and that having huge football players on the gridiron adds to the show that is professional football. Strength and performance, suggest some, make the cash registers ring. Not included in that equation of dollars and cents is the impressionable audience watching them. As Donald Hooton testified, "I am tired of hearing you tell us that kids should not look up to you as role models. If you haven't figured it out yet, let me break the news to you, you are role models whether you like it or not. And parents across America should hold you accountable for behavior that inspires our kids to do things that put their health at risk and teaches them that the ethics we try to teach them at home somehow don't apply to you."

Unfortunately, some of these "role models" have a very vested interest in not being tested for steroids, or keeping the penalties almost nonexistent. Huge salaries and lucrative endorsement deals typically go hand in hand with record-breaking seasons. And is it likely that ownership will take an adamant stand against steroids if they think the drugs are contributing to a team's success?

The National Football League is considered to have the toughest steroid testing policy in major league sports, but as recent inquiries have shown the NFL has a long way to go if they really are serious about putting an end to players using steroids and performance-enhancing drugs. In 2005 the CBS show "60 Minutes Wednesday" documented that three Carolina Panthers players were given steroid prescriptions by a South Carolina doctor within two weeks of playing in the Super Bowl in February of 2004.

The NFL boasts that it conducts nearly 10,000 tests every year for steroids and performance enhancing drugs, but in a sport where experts in steroid abuse such as Charles Yesalis (Penn State Professor and editor of *Anabolic Steroids in Sports and Exercise*) have categorized usage as "epidemic," how is it that only 54 players have been suspended since steroid testing began in 1989? And of those 54 players, how is it possible that so few, if any, have been "stars?"

Until 2005, in order for an NFL player to test positive for steroids that individual had to have a greater than 6:1 ratio of testosterone to epitestosterone (a natural hormone found in the human body). In typical testing, the ratio of testosterone to epitestosterone in the average human is 1:1. Given that kind of latitude, it is no wonder that players could use testosterone with impunity. Belatedly (and pending approval of the NFL Players Association), the NFL has now announced the new ratio for a failed test to be 4:1.

There are many who say the problem is in the testing itself. The NFL, MLB, and NBA are in charge of their own testing, which some liken to the fox being put in charge of the hen house. Some are suspicious that the collection of the samples is flawed and they question the efficacy of having the test results controlled by the leagues (the NFL sends its drug samples to UCLA's Olympic Analytical Laboratory, identifying each sample with a number instead of a name – a situation that some believe makes it easy for the league to protect its "stars").

According to statistics from a December 2004 article in *USA Today* there were only 10 players who weighed over

300 pounds in 1986, whereas in 2004 the NFL had over 350 players topping 300 pounds. In less than twenty years players have dramatically increased in muscle and weight. I find this both incredible and inexplicable. French fries can't be credited with that inconceivable weight gain.

Personally, I am sick of all the speculation, and I'm not alone. A *USA Today*/CNN poll conducted in 2002 showed that 86% of baseball fans agreed that players should be tested for steroids. Isn't it time to dispel suspicion about tainted performers and performances? We have to send a message to our young people that cheaters and cheating aren't tolerated. There is a name for any superstar who uses steroids. He or she is called a felon.

The tacit support of steroid use in professional sports, the winking and looking the other way, has sent a terrible message to our youth. Children have died trying to emulate their sports heroes. Instead of sending out a message to "play fair," our kids are instead being taught ways to "beat the system."

The Bay Area Laboratory Cooperative – better known as BALCO – is a company being accused of helping athletes to try and beat the system. BALCO founder Victor Conte and three other men are awaiting trial in U.S. District Court in San Francisco on steroid conspiracy charges. The ramifications have extended far beyond San Francisco, though. So-called "San Francisco Gate" reared itself at the 2004 Greek Olympics when Kostas Kenteris (defending 200 meter gold medal winner) and Katerina Thanou (defending silver medalist) failed to report for their drug tests (their claim was that they suffered a motorcycle accident – a report that the media pounced upon – stories around the world appeared which stated the real reason was the fear of those tests revealing the use of performance enhancing drugs).

The unraveling of BALCO started to occur in the summer of 2003 when a track coach turned in a syringe half full of the "clear" – a name Conte gave to one of his drugs (the reason Conte called his THG "the clear" was because at the time no drug tests could detect its presence. Athletes came to him thinking they could cheat and get away with it). The syringe was given to the United States Anti-Doping Agency (USADA), and they were able to determine its chemical structure, a previously unknown steroid called tetrahydrogestrinone (THG for short). The scope of the THG problem showed itself on October 16, 2003 when USADA retested urine samples from the national track and field champions the previous June and found several positives for THG.

As the BALCO ball of yarn has continued to unravel, more of the story has unfolded. In a television interview conducted with Conte on ABC's *20/20* in December of 2004, the founder of BALCO admitted tailoring drug regimens for top athletes including Marion Jones, Kelli White and Tim Montgomery. He also went on to explain how his products had found their way into the hands of football (Conte said Bill Romanowski of the Oakland Raiders was his first client) and baseball stars (he said drugs from BALCO's labs ended up in the hands of Jason Giambi and Barry Bonds).

During the interview Conte said that getting around anti-doping rules is "like taking candy from a baby," and that, "In short, the Olympic games are a fraud." According to

Conte, steroids in professional sports are more than widespread. "Let me tell you the biggest joke of all," he said during the interview. "I would guesstimate that more than 50 percent of the athletes are taking some form of anabolic steroids."

I don't like sports being a fraud. I don't like "champions" taking illegal substances to help them win or perform better, but this behavior is only going to stop if the fans demand it. Athletes will continue to abuse steroids, human growth hormone, EPO (an acronym for erythropoietin, a hormone which boosts red blood cells and increases endurance), insulin, and other "stealth drugs" unless the penalties are so severe as to discourage usage. We should be talking about "career ending drugs" instead of career ending injuries. There needs to be more than a stigma attached to steroids. The threat of an asterisk isn't enough. The threat of a lifetime ban from a sport might be just the antidote we need to end steroid use in professional athletes.

Major league sports needs to have an outside agency policing their own house. In 1999 the World Anti-Doping Committee (WADA) was set up to drug test Olympic athletes for performance enhancing substances. In the year 2000 the United States set up its own version of WADA, creating the U.S. Anti-Doping Agency (USADA). Track and field athletes call the procedures used by WADA and USADA as "knock and pee." Testers can arrive at any time during the night or day, and when they do athletes have to provide a urine sample. There is no privacy. The athlete disrobes from the waist down and provides a sample while the tester watches.

"Knock and pee" would not be popular with professional athletes. They have already complained about the "invasion of privacy" associated with steroid testing. I say, "Tough luck." Maybe there are only a few bad apples in professional sports, or maybe, as some think, the apple is already rotten to the core. Steroid testing will tell us the state of professional sports, or perhaps guide athletes into the right decisions. The only way we're going to change the potential of steroid abuse in major league sports is by having random testing conducted any time, any place, any where. That means off-season and on-season. That means you pee in a cup right in front of somebody. And that means if you fail the test you pay a severe price.

As Donald Hooton said to the congressional committee, "Right to privacy? What about our rights as parents – our rights to expect that the adults that our kids all look up to will be held to a standard that does not include behavior that is dangerous, felonious, and is cheating?"

The penalties are going to have to get serious too, and they're going to have to be retroactive. No one can think they're going to get away with a stealth drug just because the tests might not have yet caught up with the chemists. Is it wrong to demand a lifetime ban from a sport for using steroids? I don't think so. Professional athletes face lifetime bans for betting on sports. Fay Vincent, former Major League Baseball commissioner, was asked if the BALCO scandal was worse for baseball than the Pete Rose gambling scandal. Vincent said, "Was World War II worse than World War I? They're both bad."

The owners of professional sports franchises will only start to listen if the fans show their disapproval. We have that power. We can boycott games and not watch or listen to sporting events. If fans show they are serious about not wanting professional athletes taking steroids (and polls indicate that this is overwhelmingly the case), then we have to get that message across to ownership, players, and governing boards. A level playing field shouldn't be a goal but an absolute necessity, and we need to act accordingly.

I also agree with Senator Bunning. Forget about an asterisk. If Ben Johnson could lose his gold medal to steroids, then professional athletes should be similarly penalized. At this time, athletes are tempted to take steroids because there are very few repercussions. The penalties, for the most part, are a joke. That must change.

If we have to pull some athletes off of their pedestals, I consider that a small price for sending a message that our young people will see and hear. No one is above the law, and we have to make that clear.

By cleaning up professional sports, I would expect a "trickle down effect" to college and high school sports. The specter of harsh penalties and vigorous testing might dissuade younger athletes from even considering steroids or other performance enhancing drugs. If high school and college athletes know that professional teams are testing for steroids, and that these tests might reveal prior unacceptable usage that would preclude a player's being drafted, the temptation to use steroids might disappear. Furthermore, because of steroids, unrealistic bars have been set for athletic performance. Without steroids, the bar would once again drop to being attainable without drugs.

Steroids aren't acceptable. They're not "cool." They almost killed me and they have killed others. I thought they would make me strong but they made me weak. That's why my mission is to get rid of steroids on and off the field.

You might argue that people still smoke even though they know that it is not good for them. While that is true, public perception about smoking has changed. No one thinks it's glamorous any more. Most of those who do smoke acknowledge that it's a filthy habit. Smiling stars and athletes no longer puff for the camera or magazine cover. As a consequence, smoking has declined.

We can do the same thing with steroids. We can superimpose in people's minds an image of a skeleton over huge muscles. We can get the message out to young people that steroids aren't worth it. I am not naïve enough to think that education will totally eradicate the use of steroids, but we need to make the images of Taylor Hooton and Rob Garibaldi and others who have fallen to steroids just as prominent as the overblown image of steroid-using sports stars.

Steroid use means a body to die for – we need to convince our kids that this is a risk not worth taking!

About the Author

Using anabolic steroids almost killed Jeff Rutstein. For three and a half years he was addicted to these illegal drugs. When he gave up steroids, Jeff's life went into a tailspin from which he took more than a year to recover. As he crawled out of the abyss Jeff had an epiphany: he wanted to work with people who were in trouble – be it substance abuse, stress, or psychological despair – and help them surmount their problems. What saved Jeff – a system of exercises he calls Mindful Movements – he wanted to bring to other people.

In 1990 Jeff started Custom Fitness in Boston, a center that promotes a mind-body approach to exercise. Jeff's unique approach to fitness is the opposite of the usual "no pain no gain" workout mills. He quickly gained converts throughout the Boston area with doctors and mental health professionals recommending their clients to him. Based on his experiences, Jeff wrote *Rutstein on Fitness: Strengthening the Body to Heal the Mind*.

Jeff was named Distinguished Personal Trainer by *American Fitness*, an Outstanding Fitness Leader by *Reebok Instructor News*, The Best Samaritan by *American Health*, and is a Master Level Personal Trainer certified by the International Dance and Exercise Association (IDEA).

His revolutionary approach to fitness, and his own life story, has resulted in Jeff's being featured in more than 100 national and international media outlets, including CNN, NBC, ABC, *The Washington Post, Reuters, The Boston Globe*, and others.